Master of Illusion
Written by Frater Iosis

First paperback edition February 23, 2023.

Cover design by

ISBN 978-1-951434-86-1 (paperback)

Published by Illuminist Books
Illuminism.net

"Religion is an illusion and it derives its strength from the fact that it falls in with our instinctual desires."

-Sigmund Freud

MASTER OF ILLUSION

Written by:
FRATER IOSIS

This work is based on the research and personal gnosis of Frater Iosis. This purpose of this book is only to create a spark in the mind of the reader. Discovering the content as fact will only come from within as the consciousness awakens to reality. Veritas Excelsior!

Table of Contents

Master of Illusion

INTRODUCTION

We live in an age of opinions. An age where the wondrous teachings of the ancients has been corrupted and lost. People all over the world assume they understand the methods of attaining knowledge, if not believe they already have acquired it. The mass mind has fantastical ideas of aliens, secret cabals, and organized witchcraft used against them, as fact. The internet is filled with self-help gurus teaching falsities only to earn ad revenue. The magical gifts of psychic and other occult powers are claimed to be possessed by multitudes of people. This is, as hard as it is to accept, all a result of degeneration and devolution.

Where are the great people of our age? Where is the modern-day Albert Einstein, Plato, Pythagoras, Michelangelo, Beethoven? They do not exist. Why is that? Who, living in this time, can we say is of the stature and magnitude of those great individuals who lived in prior times? No one. Why is this?

Despite the public opinion that mankind is so much more advanced than those of earlier times, where are the great people?
Are we, in fact, so far advanced than those who lived in earlier times? No. We are not.

We are far behind them. The knowledge, wisdom, and skills that individuals possessed in the past was far superior to the current times. All the technology that we have and say is highly advanced, is in fact because of those great minds that graced the civilization before us. We cannot accept the credit for any of it.

In the previous eras, those individuals, as well as many others, were fascinated by the esoteric and occult teachings of the mind, body, and spirit. They interested themselves in applied psychology, in understanding occult teachings of the nature and capability of man. This desire to learn these concepts and teachings propelled them to better themselves to the point where they were capable of doing the great work that they did.

Today this is not the case. The mass mind is not interested in these things any longer. It is interested in superficial things and lives solely in their imagination. Even the religions of the world, which were very strong and growing years ago, are now used for nothing other than material for jokes and subject to mockery and angst.

The evolution of man requires an upward movement from the level of religion and not a downward fall from it. The mass mind has done the latter. It has fallen from the

beginnings of understanding religion to land
in a cloud of imagination. This imagination,
combined with arrogance and idealism, has
led us to where we are now – in an age of
opinions.

Opinions, as we know, are nothing more than
statements of how we feel about something,
with no factual basis or understanding. From
the mass mind to the world governments, to
those that "instruct" us online, there is
nothing more than mere opinion.

Who would waste their precious time with
these opinions? Well, only those who don't
value their time in the first place. And who are
those that value time? They are the ones who
understand what the goal of this existence is,
and those who desire to complete that goal in
this life, without waiting a second longer. That
is only a small handful of people. A very small
handful.

The others seek for comforts, for luxuries,
and all the superficial derivatives of them.
Very few people seek knowledge. Even
though they have heard the saying, knowledge
is power, they do not seek it. They believe.
Everything. How can you believe anything in
the world we live in? Has it not crossed your
mind when you see the character of those
who govern? Has it not crossed your mind

when you think about the world situation? The situation of the people - suffering, struggling, and miserable. The people are the reason for all the things that the world and its people are experiencing. The population experiences the manifestation of the mass mind. Until the mass mind changes, this will continue to be the situation on the planet. However, the mass mind cannot and will not ever change altogether. These are individual works. But always remember that what one person does, has an impact on the whole.

That is the concept of the microcosm and the macrocosm.

In this book, I will explain some of the facets of illusion and then contrast them with the reality of the situation. Now, you may ask yourself, after reading this Introduction, "well, why should I believe you, if this is the age of opinions?" Good question. You should think that. I am not trying to get you to think something, as that is a useless effort. I am only writing certain things with the hope that whoever is meant to read this will gain a spark of interest to investigate and experience the concepts further. I am not trying to teach anything to you. I am only trying to create a small spark.

This is a very tricky book to write. The reason being that explaining these subjects to the mass mind is seemingly pointless. And the ones who are not of the mass mind, those who are on a path to wisdom, wouldn't need to read this book, because they already know the content.

In any case, I present you this work. May it bring only a positive change, however small, to your mind and life. Veritas Excelsior!

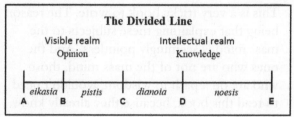

Figure 1 Divided Line by Plato – supplied at the end of Book 6 of The Republic.

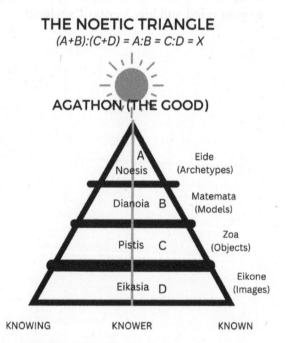

Figure 2 The Noetic Triangle

CHAPTER 1

The Perception of Reality in Relation to Noetics and the Divine Dialectic

Reality, in spiritual terms, is a vast topic. One that must be only considered until it can be fully understood.

It is very common in Eastern spiritual texts to hear about the subject of maya[1]. It is frequently referred to in books written by Swamis and theosophists[2], however, it is not clear as to its true meaning. From the standpoint of western occultism, Noesis[3], or clear vision, is what gives us the true view of reality. All the other states of consciousness below Noesis do not provide one with a "clear vision" of reality. This poses a relatively difficult issue in that it is impossible to view reality for what it actually is until you have reached a particular state of being, or level of consciousness. This issue makes writing this

---

[1] Hinduism: 1. The supernatural power wielded by gods and demons to produce illusions. 2. The power by which the universe becomes manifest; the illusion or appearance of the phenomenal world.

[2] Anyone who believes any philosophy maintaining that a knowledge of God may be achieved through spiritual ecstasy, direct intuition, and special relations.

[3] The fourth and highest level on consciousness; clear-vision.

book especially difficult since I am trying to explain something to the reader which can only be fully understood once you really have no need for this book. However, I will try to elucidate certain concepts and ideas that, in the past, have not been quite clearly explained by authors writing about them. Hopefully this book will provide enough food for thought on these concepts at the reader's current level of understanding, whatever it may be. And once the reader has achieved a higher state of being, this book will become perfectly understood through all its levels.

The Divine Dialectic[4] or Noetic Triangle[5] which represents the four states of consciousness, is the best diagrammatic representation of the journey of consciousness the human being must endure to reach the state of clear vision, or Noesis, that western esotericism or occultism has produced. As you may know, almost the entire population of people on Earth reside in either the first level of consciousness, Eikasia[6], or the border zone of the first and second level, Pistis[7]. In the past, there were more people residing in the second level of Pistis than there are today. This is a result of

---

[4] See illustration 1 and 2.
[5] Diagrammatic display of the four levels of consciousness.
[6] The lowest plane of consciousness; where most people are.
[7] The second level of consciousness;

devolution, which is the natural process of all organisms. With the slow but albeit sure disappearance of religion, mankind is devolving from Pistis to Eikasia. Eikasia, is the level of imagination. It is nothing more. There is no factual perception of reality in Eikasia. The untrained and uncontrolled mind is what rules and the sense impressions received by the person is what dictates the images produced by the imagination. This manufactured imagination is what is then "believed" by the person and thought of as either a strong opinion or fact. This, in reality, is not even close to being true. And there is no case where the imagination will produce, by chance, the true reality, because the true reality is something that cannot be seen until certain occult organs and processes are functioning correctly. Despite these facts, the imagination is what is considered "knowledge" in the state of Eikasia.

So, this is where the consciousness of mankind is dwelling. This is what is erroneously referred to as the collective consciousness[8]. This should not be called the collective consciousness, as that consciousness is actually referring to something entirely different. It should be

---

[8] The set of shared beliefs, ideas and moral attitudes which operate as a unifying force within society. Other names for this are hive mind, group mind, mass mind, and social mind.

called the mass mind. We will discuss the correct meaning of the collective consciousness in a later chapter.

In this realm of imagination, called Eikasia, we see many people who are imagining that they possess psychic powers, and some advanced level of spiritual understanding. This is also erroneous. The powers that they think they have and the knowledge that they assume they possess is based on the imagination of those individuals, not actual fact. These people, who believe their imagination, then continue to preach and "teach" others and use their imaginary psychic gifts to make money and "help" others who are also living in the realm of imagination, and this creates only stronger opinions and illusions of more and more people. It is a one-way street, leading to a dead end.

In reality, the advanced levels of understanding and psychic powers that so many claim to have, can only be achieved by proven progression along the spiritual path. The spiritual path is not forgiving and does not change. It has been outlined by the ancient masters and the same map can be used today for the same purpose. There is no way around it. It must be done to unveil the knowledge within the consciousness, and the psychic gifts that one can obtain.

The perception of reality along the progression upwards of the Noetic Triangle is something that unfolds in a slow, but sure manner. This happens when the student is actively conscious in the process. The student will understand that ideas and concepts understood a particular way will help him or her on the path in their specific state and then again be revisited in the higher states of consciousness, but understood not differently, but more acutely than in the previous. In Eastern occultism, this is commonly referred to as "peeling the onion". The more layers you peel, the more you will understand. It is the same concept. So, we must understand that each level of consciousness is going to give us a more acute understanding of the same ideas and concepts that we have come across previously. For example, in Eikasia, the person will be guided by their imagination, influenced by impressions received. In Pistis, the images projected by the imagination take on a very definite shape, which is commonly seen as religious representations of deities. In Dianoia[9], we see those images of deities disregarded since they cannot be proven scientifically, and in Noesis, we see them for what they truly are.

---

[9] The third level of consciousness.

The most important thing to remember is that until our consciousness rises to the level of clear vision or Noesis, we cannot, in any way shape, or form, see the truth of anything. We cannot perceive reality and any attempt at trying to describe it or decipher it, is in fact, not going to be accurate. However, this does not stop anyone from doing so.

A quick search online will reveal to us that several people, from the wealthy and famous to the average person, always make attempts at trying to describe reality. We often hear ideas of the possibility of living in a simulation, extra-terrestrial involvement, etc.

To the occult student, all these opinions should be discarded as easily as used napkins because unless the person stating these ideas is a being who is residing in Noesis, they are impossible.

In the great magical text, The Arbatel of Magic [Veterum][10], we read early on that there are two types of knowledge. One that can be gained from studying and learning, and the other, a more special kind, which can only be obtained by the grace of the Gods. The perception of reality falls under the second

---

[10] English translation: Arbatel: On the Magic of the Ancients, a Latin grimoire on Renaissance ceremonial magic published in 1575 in Switzerland.

type of knowledge. It is a knowledge that is related only to the consciousness and not to the parts of the brain that say, mathematics, is. This knowledge, because it is related to the consciousness, can only be obtained by the occult methods of opening the parts of the consciousness which are related to the great spiritual paths described by ancient sages and occultists.

These occult methods are very precise and very clear. There is no room for debate and no shortcuts. It is a way of living. This way of living must be followed to bear its fruits. Currently, mankind in general is not living in this fashion, and does not even know that this is the reason for living this way. Mankind, in general, disregards the wisdom of the ancients and the great art of magic as nothing more than foolery, as a result of their dwelling in Eikasia.

As time progresses, the disappearance of these maps of life will prove a huge detriment to the spiritual evolution of mankind.

As one climbs the Noetic Triangle, one will raise the consciousness from imagination to religion to science to reality. This means that the previous three levels provide nothing special and nothing that the occultists of the past who have reached the level of Noesis already knew.

Mankind, even with their technological advancements, are still vastly far behind the ancient occultists. Even though this is the case, because of the advancements in technology, man thinks that he is much more advanced than past civilizations and getting better every day. This is itself a clearly erroneous view due to the lack of living the way the masters have taught and the occult books have outlined. This is itself proof that the consciousness of the general population resides in Eikasia, as their delusions of grandeur are simply in their imagination.

Earlier, I spoke of impressions received by the person which are influencing the imagination. What are these impressions and where do they come from? These impressions are correctly called 'sense impressions'. The five senses that we possess are receivers of these impressions. Everything we see, hear, touch, taste and smell leaves an impression on the subconscious mind. We begin receiving these impressions from the time we are in our mother's womb. The subconscious mind then takes these impressions and begins to grow them, even though we are unaware of this in most cases. Consider these forgotten impressions as weeds in a garden. We don't

really see them in the beginning, but once they
grow large enough, they become a nuisance
and start to disrupt the garden we have
consciously planted. These "weeds" are what
lead to the addictions, and other problems
that we encounter in our life. And it requires a
great deal of work to clean out the garden of
the mind. The ideal situation is to not let these
weeds grow in the first place. This is done by
protecting ourselves from certain impressions,
and that requires prudence.

So, back to the impressions. Our eyes are
probably the strongest receivers of
impressions, and everything we see leaves a
powerful imprint on our subconscious minds.
Things such as movies are very powerful and
can greatly assist the mind in the creation of
its imagination. Our minds can be so guided
by subtle concepts found in movies, that a
person can very easily begin to equate things
that are found in movies, with the world he
lives in. Thus, the imagination is fueled, and
the illusion of reality grows more powerful in
Eikasia. In Eastern texts, when we read the
great Masters saying things like, "We must
detach the senses," we should understand that
as relating to the impressions I have just
discussed. Since the senses are the receivers of
these impressions, the detachment of them
would provide a more realistic grip on our
lives. In the Western world, the stimulation of

senses is so abundant that it is very difficult to live without being saturated by these impressions. Escaping to nature is a much better way to go, however not practical for most people. So, we must be consciously aware of what impressions we are willing to receive if we wish to continue upwards on the path of evolving the consciousness.

There are several conspiracy theories that have been created and propagated by these impressions. Millions of people support these theories because they too, have been saturated by the same impressions and their collective imagination provides a great deal of fuel for such illusion. Regarding the levels of consciousness, it is also important to know that people who reside on higher levels can sufficiently control those on lower levels if they possess a proper understanding of how the mind works. Obviously, a person residing in the highest level of Noesis, would not do such things, as they would seem pointless, but those on the other levels would surely be capable. For example, if there were people on the level of Dianoia[11] (the level of science), it would be easy to influence those on the Eikasia level since they would be able to create the correct impressions in the mind to

---

[11] The third level of consciousness, above Pistis, and below Noesis.

fuel whatever they want planted in the subconsciousness. Just an example.

Science, as occultists know, describes the least of everything. It is a very crude and mundane explanation of things. The consciousness still eludes even the greatest scientists and always will. This is simply because there is a clear line of demarcation in the consciousness between science and reality. The reality of things is much more different from what anyone who cannot see it would understand. It is something like an icy glass. As the ice melts, the glass becomes more and more transparent. Eikasia is the frozen glass. Pistis is frosted. Dianoia is the melting frost running down the glass and Noesis is the pure, clear glass. The view through the glass will always be distorted until it reaches the Noetic state.

The Divided Line

The Divided Line of the Dialectic, as described by Plato[12], is separated into two sections, the Visible World, and the Intelligible World.

Eikasia and Pistis are located in the Visible World and this world produces two types of knowledge, illusion (Eikasia) and belief

---

[12] Ancient Greek philosopher born during the Greek Classical Era.

(Pistis). The illusion of Eikasia is the illusion of our ordinary, everyday experiences. The belief of Pistis is of discrete physical objects which cast their shadow. The natural sciences are included in the level of Pistis.

According to Plato, Eikasia, was referring to a human way of dealing with appearances. Something that we will also discuss at length in a later chapter.

The combination of Eikasia and Pistis add up to something called Doxa. Doxa is a common belief or popular opinion and can be contrasted with something called Episteme[13], which is knowledge. The term, doxa, is ancient Greek and comes from the verb dokein which means to appear, to seem, to think, to accept. Doxa is seen as a belief, unrelated to reason, that resides in the unreasoning, lower parts of the soul. The collective imagination of people residing in Eikasia is doxa. This is apparently what most people imagine the collective consciousness is.

Plato indicates the concept of doxasta, which summarizes that physical objects are manifestations of doxa and thus not in their true form. This applies to all physical objects.

---

13 Knowledge. Specifically intellectual certain knowledge.

Doxa is the opponent to knowledge and leads to the classical opposition of error to truth. Plato said that this has become a major concern in Western Philosophy.

On a side note, the word *democracy* is defined, too, as the manifestation of public opinion.

Eikasia has several interpretations. One is the inability to perceive whether a perception is an image of something else. This is immensely important to consider as it would reveal the reason as to why people cannot understand allegory, particularly in spiritual and philosophical contexts.

In the Intelligible World, there are 2 subdivisions, Dianoia, and Noesis. Dianoia is where the soul uses the figures given by the former division as images. This can be only hypothetical and instead of going upwards to a principle, it descends to the other end. An example of this is mathematical reasoning. Noesis is where the soul passes out of hypotheses and goes upwards to a principle above hypothesis, making no use of images as in Dianoia. It, instead, creates ideas.

Examine the summaries of each state of consciousness below to get a better general understanding:

Noesis – *Affection of the Psyche:* Knowledge (understanding): understanding of only the intelligible. *Type of object:* Only ideas, which are all given existence and truth by the Good Itself. *Method of Psyche:* The Psyche examines all hypotheses by the Dialectic making no use of likeness, always moving towards a First Principle. *Relative Reality:* Highest.

Dianoia - *Affection of the Psyche:* Knowledge (thought): thought that recognizes but is not only of the intelligible. *Type of object:* Some ideas, specifically those of Geometry and Number. *Method of Psyche:* The Psyche assumes hypotheses while making use of likeness, always moving towards final conclusions. *Relative Reality:* High.

Pistis - *Affection of the Psyche:* Opinion (belief): belief concerning visible things. *Type of object:* visible things. *Method of Psyche:* The eye makes probable predictions upon observing visible things. *Relative Reality:* Low.

Eikasia - *Affection of the Psyche:* Opinion (imagination): conjecture concerning likeness. *Type of object:* likeness of visible things. *Method of Psyche:* The eye makes guesses upon observing likeness of visible things. *Relative Reality:* Lowest.

Plato's Allegory of the Cave

The Allegory of the Cave, presented in Plato's
work, The Republic, was done to compare the
effect of education and the lack of it in our
nature. In this allegory, Plato describes a
group of people who have lived chained to
the wall of a cave all their lives, facing a blank
wall. The people watch shadows projected on
the wall from objects passing in front of a fire
behind them and give names to these
shadows. The shadows are the prisoners'
reality, but are not accurate representations of
the real world. The shadows represent the
fragment of reality that we can normally
perceive through our senses, while the objects
under the sun represent the true forms of
objects we can perceive only through reason.

All of these things point us to one
understanding. That is the different levels of
"knowledge" and how they affect our
perception of reality. As we can see, only the
level of Noesis is revealing the highest level of
relative truth and reality to us. We can also see
the progression of imagination-based opinion
to understanding-based knowledge.

Religion falls under the level of Pistis. It is
associated with the belief, but still opinion,
regarding visible things. It is dependent on
likeness and the person makes probable

predictions upon observing these images. This is why we have a divided opinion on the existence of God. The predictions made differ in groups. But this is also the reason why religion is an important step in everyone's journey. It is a necessary step to take in order to rise above the minimal understanding it provides and those who reach the higher levels of consciousness will then understand its true meaning and purpose in our lives.

To summarize, we are concerned with epistemology and ontology[14]. Epistemology[15] is considered a subfield of philosophy, along with others such as ethics, logic, and metaphysics. All of these are part of the applied religious philosophy of Illuminism.

This is the journey. To understand reality, we must evolve the consciousness to the level of Noesis so that we can clearly see. You will then see how your ideas on reality evolve and change along the way.

---

[14] The philosophical study of being, as well as related concepts such as existence, becoming, and reality.

[15] From the Ancient Greek episteme meaning knowledge. Means the theory of knowledge and is a branch of philosophy dealing with knowledge.

CHAPTER 2

The Two Key Components to Understand in Evolution

The evolution of the consciousness has two key components that are of vital importance to understand, sex and psychology.

Sex and psychology, although seemingly different, are greatly intertwined, and the understanding of their connection is one of the most important things you can learn. The proper understanding of these two topics and their connection is necessary to the unveiling of one of the greatest occult mysteries.

Sex

On the topic of sex, a correct understanding of the processes in the body and the mental catalysts are key.

The sexual current is the creation current in the human being. It is the power of the Gods and is capable, as you know, of creating life. With this basic knowledge, we have to be aware also of the meaning of the word life. Life, as used above, is referring to a physical life, but there is another type of life that exists. To the occultists, there is another type of birth, a spiritual life. The spiritual life is birthed when the spiritual child is born. The spiritual child is not a physical child, but a different type of being. It is a being comprised of knowledge and wisdom and must be born within one's own self. This birth requires the energy from the same sexual current.

If we study the Qabalah[16], we understand that all physical objects and beings are not originally created in the physical plane or Malkuth[17] (earth). They are created in higher dimensions and then, for the sake of this statement, condensate, into physical form, through the dimensions. The physical form is the last of the transformations to take place in these dimensions. Just as a physical human being is created in the higher dimensions and then condenses down to Malkuth, if we stop the process in a higher dimension, we can birth the spiritual child.

This process requires the use of the Arcanum Arcanorum[18] or the Greatest Mystery. It is a sexual mystery and it explains how to create a

---

[16] An esoteric method, discipline and school of thought in Jewish mysticism.
[17] Means kingdom. Associated with the realm of matter/earth or the physical world.
[18] The Mystery of Mysteries

spiritual child, meaning precisely a child in the higher realms, which is not physical.

The sexual fluid does not exist in a liquid form in the human body. Instead, it is in a gaseous form. The movement of this gas can be directed to different places in the body. The appearance of this substance in the liquid form is something that only happens once it descends into Malkuth.

So, we can understand that the sexual drive is first created in the mind and then activates certain areas within the body. After that state, it is in a gaseous form until it is released. The release of the substance is strictly a gratification of the sense organs and nothing necessary or positive for the fulfilling of the spiritual work.

When it is still within the body, the gas can be directed through certain physical movements and mental control. This is the basis of Kundalini[19] Yoga. Kundalini Yoga[20] describes the ancient processes of directing the flow of this gas to energize certain centers of the body and mind. This is in line with the spiritual work. So, as we can see, our correct

---

[19] Sanskrit term meaning coiled. Divine feminine energy.
[20] A specific type of yoga focused on awakening awareness.

understanding of sex is necessary to proceed along the path.

The control of the sexual energy is a key component to the spiritual work. But this control is not possible without the understanding of the mind and how our psychology is connected to the sexual drive and energy that we have.

The blood and the sexual fluids are occult substances which hold magical properties. The astral substance is found here and this is the special substance which can be used for creative purposes, if we know how to use it.

There is a phrase, Ath Ha-Adam in Hebrew which, when commonly translated, means "the man". If we write it as Ath Ha-Dam, which use the same letters, we see it translated as "the blood". Adam, allegorically is related to the blood. We can also see this in one of the alternate translations of Adam, which is *red*. This has to do with the transformation of blood which takes place during the course of spiritual evolution. So, as we can see the blood is a very important part of the occult process as well. Nietzsche wrote, "write with blood and you will know what spirit is".

All of the religions were given to us to teach us a new kind of sexual creation. A type of sexual creation far beyond that of the animal nature. This type of creation requires willpower, knowledge, and the emergence of a new kind of mind and a new kind of being. This is what is encoded into the allegories of the religions of the world. The general population of mankind, because of their residence in Eikasia, do not see this. They read the texts as if they are historical documents and not instructions.

All of the wrong thinking, and degeneration that we can attribute to mankind, is due to the overpowering animal nature of man and its overpowering of the weak-minded individuals. If you look closely, you can see this everywhere.

Mankind has forgotten that every single action has an equal and opposite reaction. And their accumulated actions regarding sex in the animal form, have created a vortex of opposite reactions damning and degenerating the entire civilization.

The evolution of the consciousness towards Noesis will never occur unless the attitude and actions towards sex changes. There is no planetary alignment or coming "age" that will take mankind to enlightenment. The correct actions are required.

Psychology

If you understood the section above on sex properly, we don't even need to address the psychology separately. But we will add a few more notes here, regardless.

The psychology of the general population as we know, is called doxa. It is the public opinion and what everyone basically thinks and does. So, in regards to sexuality, if the doxa regarding this is totally wrong, then the aspirant must do the opposite.

This is why there is no collective evolution or mass awakening as some have very ignorantly stated. It is not possible for the mass mind to understand these concepts at the same time. This is an individual journey and until each person recognizes the primary cause of the degeneration and illusion and begins to change it, nothing will happen.

Our psychology is greatly affected by the doxa. We may feel that we think differently to other people. In reality, most people do not. They are still completely influenced by the doxa. As we discussed earlier, doxa influences the subconscious mind in a very subtle way. So, it requires prudence to prevent the influence.

Initiating yourself onto the spiritual path and following it strictly is the only way to begin to unravel the web that each one of us are in. In this way, it is very important not to listen to those who live like everyone else. It is only valuable to experience things for yourself. Gnosis[21] is the key, not learning from others who are preaching things that they do not know or understand. If one who lives in an illusion tries to explain something to you, then what they are explaining is also illusion.

What we are stating above is that there is no knowledge available to anyone being taught by someone unless they are at the stage of Noesis. That being the case, only experiential knowledge which one can undergo by themselves is what is the true teacher.

---

[21] Experiential knowledge of spiritual mysteries.

CHAPTER 3

The Kundalini: The Axis of Understanding

The Kundalini is the lever of consciousness by which the individual realizes their oneness with everything. The creative impetus, which emanates from the divine, is communicated through the Kundalini, the serpent power as it is called, to the six chakras and their connection. Normally the Kundalini is sleeping a trance-like sleep, and when it is awakened from this slumber and made to work, the aspirant perceives all supernatural truths. These "supernatural" truths are the removal of illusions and the realizing of reality. The resurrection of the soul from the grave of untruth becomes an actual fact, and perception of beauty, which is an attribute of the Self, fills his heart with joy. Health is also said to be another gift of the Kundalini awakening. Swami Vivekananda[22] states in his book, Raja Yoga, that the center where all residual sensations are, as it were, stored up is called the Muladhara[23] Chakra. This is very

[22] A Hindu monk, philosopher and chief disciple of Sri Ramakrishna.
[23] The foundation of the physical structure of the body. Located at the base of the spine.

interesting to note since we have previously discussed the need to detach from the senses. What this indicates is that all the impressions that we have received have sent their doxa-related sensations to the Muladhara Chakra. This area of built-up sensations is what helps to bring about the untamed sexual impulses.

The Kundalini, however, is, as Swami Vivekananda states, the individual bodily representative of the great Cosmic Power (Shakti) which creates and sustains the universe. If we remember from chapter one, we came across the word "maya". In the footnotes, the definition was placed and states that maya is the (1) supernatural power wielded by the gods and demons to produce illusions; (2) the power by which the universe becomes manifest; (3) the illusion or appearance of the phenomenal world. This would suggest that maya and Shakti are intricately connected. They are connected in that Shakti is the producer (and inversely, the destroyer) of maya. This power of Shakti is latent and dormant in the Kundalini. When the Kundalini is not awakened, we are blinded by illusion. When the Kundalini is awakened, we are exposed to reality. This also indicates that the powers that we call supernatural are really the use and revealing of the illusion itself.

The Kundalini is said to be lying dormant guarding the opening of the passage that leads to the seat of Brahma. This seat is said to be Brahma-randhra, that is the ventricular cavity in the brain. This communicates the ventricles of the brain with the channel in the spinal cord (Sushumna-nadi) and the subarachnoid space (akasha). So, the dormant Kundalini is guarding these three important openings in the cerebro-spinal nervous system. This means that unless it is awakened, or made consciously active, one cannot send one's embodied soul (Jivatma), along the Sushumna-nadi to the Brahma-randhra nor is he able to assist the soul captured in the Randhra, to be freed to join the Universal Soul (Paramatma) outside.

This joining has to happen for the aspirant to remove the soul from bondage of the maya. The Kundalini can also be known as the cord of desire and the liberation of that desire by awakening it or making it consciously active will free oneself from bondage and desire, and thus free them from the senses.

According to Hindu ontology, these desires revert the soul to the control of Prana and Chitta (the mind-stuff), and successive rebirths are the result. This is anything but what the aspirant desires; he wants to escape this, which can only be done by tearing

asunder the cords of desire by bringing
Kundalini under control. When Kundalini is
made to obey the callings of the soul, the soul
escapes from this cavity to occupy another
cavity called Akasha, which surrounds the
brain and the spinal cord. Further, the soul,
freed from the control of Prana[24], Chitta, and
Vasana[25], lives outside the Brahma-chakra,
and is said to pervade the whole universe.

It is understood in Hindu philosophy that
Vasana is what leads an individual to
successive rebirths. To know the proper
meaning of the term, we must deal a bit with
Karma of the embodied soul, the Jivatma of a
being. The Karma of an individual is
comprised of desire (Vasana), knowledge
(Jnana), and action (Kriya). The impressions
unconsciously left on the mind by actions in
past lives (Vasana) start a current of thought,
which is conveyed to the Jivatma and is then
translated, through his agency, into actions,
good or bad. Karma is generally of three
kinds. Sanchita Karma, the outcome of
Sanskara (impressions of past lives) and
desires (Vasana), is all the accumulated and
unexhausted Karma of past lives with which
an individual is born, and which is still to bear
fruit. Prarabdha Karma is that part of the

---

[24] Sanskrit word for breath, "life force" or "vital principle".
[25] The karmic imprint which influences the present behavior of a person.

Sanchita Karma which is worked out and the result of which is made known to us in our present birth. Kriyamana Karma, either Vartaman or Agami, is that which a man is continuously hoarding up by his present and future actions. It will then be seen that the vicious circle of Vasana, by continuously forming a web around the soul, forces it to remain embodied for liberating and experiencing the past Karma. Its final emancipation then could only be achieved by putting a stop to the generation of new Karma by conquering our Vasana or desires. When this is done there is nothing left to generate new Karma and the Jivatma is liberated from successive rebirths. On this plane, the physical plane, this can only be done by controlling the Kundalini.

In summary, the conscious control of or the awakening of the Kundalini will give the aspirant control over a system which we normally have no control over. This control that is gained has a direct impact over our mental faculties and consciousness. This control is what enables us to see the reality of the world.

The downward flow of energy in the Kundalini, which is synonymous with no control, is what degenerates the mind and prevents us with all measure from the seeing the truth. This happens by building bondage between the person and the senses, thus keeping them in doxa. However, when the Kundalini energy is directed upwards and the coiled serpent awakens, it cuts through the doxa like a hot knife through butter and reveals the mysteries of life, death and existence and propels the consciousness towards Noesis.

When the Kundalini is awakened from her sleep, and willfully used, it forces a passage through the different chakras and excites them to action. This is what opens the mind and all vision and wonderful powers come to the aspirant when it reaches the brain.

The aspirant then becomes perfectly detached from the body and mind and the soul finds itself free in every respect. All the "miracles" we have heard of can be explained by this conscious control over the Kundalini.

Wrong Knowledge

Wrong knowledge is information based on false perception. The example that is often given in Asian philosophy is that while walking we can suddenly think we see a snake and because of it we experience a moment of terror until we realize that what we are seeing is just a coiled rope.

We all experience this kind of misperception. This phenomenon is related to how sensations are interpreted and translated by the psyche. This example is very simple, and one might say it is superficial, but it serves to illustrate a problem that we have all of the time, twenty-four hours a day. The problem is that we do not know how to correctly perceive. We assume that the way our mind translates information is always accurate. However, the fact is that it is never accurate. Materialistic science is proving that now.

The physicists who are studying phenomena in nature are now proving that our perceptions lie. Those scientists and doctors who study the brain, consciousness, the senses, quantum mechanics and many other topics are proving that all of us are the most insatiable liars; we lie to ourselves. We do not see what is actually in front of us: instead, we only see how our mind interprets it.

One person sees a dog and reacts with friendliness. Another person sees the same dog and reacts with disgust. Neither sees the dog for what it is. Each one only sees the response of their psychological filters.

Innumerable experiments have proven that none of us see reality. Tests have been given to rooms of hundreds of people, where all

view the same video, and none see the actual
content of the video. In one famous example,
people are told to watch a video of a group of
people tossing a ball. Everyone can watch that
and see the ball being passed, but none see
what else is happening in the video. (I won't
spoil it for you in case you also get a chance
to experience the test). Nevertheless, the fact
remains —proven, repeatedly — that we only
see through our psychological filters. We do
not really perceive objectively, or even clearly.

Yet, humanity just does not get it. Religions
and mystical traditions have been saying this
for thousands of years. Now the scientists are
saying it too, and we still do not believe it. We
cannot imagine how our perception could
possibly be wrong. But, the fact is that we do
not see things accurately.

False perception does not refer only to
mistaken perceptions of the eyes. It refers to
how you, as a psyche, perceive all things. The
type of mistaken perception that is the most
significant cause of suffering is entirely in your
mind. It is the perception of how you think
and feel.

As an example, consider two best friends
having a conversation where both people
misunderstand what is being said, and this
causes each one of them to generate negative

feelings towards the other. Then suddenly, the friendship is in doubt. Do not we all experience that all the time? Yet, still we do not recognize that the problem is not with the spouse or the friend. The problem is in our mind.

We constantly reflect on "that thing that was said" and our mind extrapolates and starts adding to it. We invent scenes. We imagine conversations. We create events, occurrences, statements. None of it is real! We think, "he said this and I know he also meant this and this and this." So we start adding lots of interpretations and additional meanings. Where does all of that come from? Who is interjecting the additional information into that event? Is it based on facts? No. Never. It is all projections of the mind. It is all modifications and "false perceptions whose real form is not seen." We are not seeing the soul or the heart of the mind of the other person. We are only seeing the projections of our own mind, and yet we believe those projections are real. We do not know where they came from or what they are about. We do not question their reality. But they are not real! The problem is that we are doing this all of the time, with everything.

What about what others have told us? Depending on who said it, we may assume

everything that was said is absolutely true.
Yet, how do we know? Do we ever really
consider how reliable the information is?

Society, education, media, books, television,
etc. all feed us huge quantities of information
that we accept as reliable knowledge. Yet,
when we consider this in light of yoga, we
have to admit that most of what we have been
told is really wrong knowledge, because it is
based on beliefs, theories, assumptions, sales
pitches, political slants, outright lies, sectarian
conflicts, resentments, etc.

Even science, assumed to be so objective and
reliable, reverses itself weekly! Last week, it
stated definitely and without any doubt that
"this is this way," then a week later, "Actually,
it is this way." Scientists have been doing this
for decades, and still do it without any loss of
self-confidence! Really, it is astonishing to
watch the scientists and doctors — how self-
assured they are — and then see them reverse
themselves shortly after, as if they never said
things were the opposite. Of course, we see
politicians and priests doing the same thing,
and all of them are supposed to be leading
society!

We cannot blame them, however, because
they suffer exactly the same condition that we
do. All of us suffer the condition of believing

that what we think and feel is based on facts, and that what we perceive is really the full extent of what can be perceived. Sadly, that is dead wrong. We do not perceive even a tiny of fraction of what can be perceived. By awakening the consciousness, we start to perceive more.

In synthesis, wrong knowledge is a painful modification, and it is the type of modification that we experience for most of our lives.

Right Knowledge (Pramana)

Right knowledge is direct perception, something that we have seen for ourselves and can confirm.

Chief among this type of perception is right knowledge of divinity, direct experience of God. Since most of us have not had that experience, we do not have right knowledge of divinity; we have wrong knowledge; we have false perceptions; we have fantasies. We think, "God must be like this or God may be like that or I do not believe in God or God is not real." All of that is wrong knowledge. Our beliefs and theories may be beautiful, but none of them are based on experience.

Right knowledge is direct perception.
Nevertheless, right knowledge, called pramana
in Sanskrit, is a modification of mind. Some
people may question how this could be.

Someone who is self-realized does not have
modifications of mind, vritis. His mind is
liberated. He does not need right knowledge
(pramana), because he is that. To say a
liberated person needs pramana (right
knowledge) is the same as saying that a flame
needs to know that is a flame. It does not. It
already is a flame, it does not need to think
that it is a flame. There is a difference
between having a thought or a mental idea of
something and knowing one is that. That is
the distinction. When you truly are something,
the thought is irrelevant and unnecessary.

Right knowledge, pramana, is a modification
of mind. It is a way of thought; it is a way of
interpreting information. It may be accurate,
but it is still an interpretation. It is not the
thing itself, but it is based on a direct
perception, or an inference, or a testimony.
We know for ourselves that it is true. Most
students have none of that about spirituality.
This is an important thing to realize.

Do not lie to yourself. If you do not have
right knowledge, if you do not have direct
perception, admit it. Do not try to convince

45

yourselves or others that you do, because you will condemn yourself to never acquire it. Be honest. If you have never been out of your body, if you have never talked face to face with your own Innermost, your Divine Mother, or an angel, or a guru-deva, good! Admit it, then work to have it, because you can. But do not lie to yourself or others. We need direct perception, but if we lie to ourselves with a false perception, then we will never have the real one.

Direct knowledge is what we ourselves have clearly perceived. Nevertheless, that does not mean that what we perceived is reality. All of us dream, and we can clearly recall what we saw, but that does not mean what we saw was real. Similarly, we can clearly observe our thoughts and feelings, but that does not make them real, reliable, or objective.

Inference is a way of knowing something is true because you have sufficient facts to support that knowledge. A simple, materialistic example would be, if you see smoke, you know there is a fire. In the same way, if you observe a negative emotion or a bad mood in yourself, you know that is not from God. That is from an ego, a defect. When you see that you are stressed or tense, that is not divinity producing that feeling. That is a conflict in your psyche between a desire and reality. That is all that stress is. You want something that you do not have. Conflict causes stress physically, emotionally, and mentally. When you recognize the desire and you deal with the desire and you disempower the desire then the stress goes away. It is really simple. That's inference: knowing something by the evidence that surrounds it.

Testimony is knowing something by a reputable source.

So, again taking this from the spiritual point of view, what do we consider to be a reputable source? It is someone or something that does have right knowledge or is an awakened master or a perfectly developed being. In this tradition, we are very strict on this point. We are exceptionally strict, because we value the soul of every person. We consider valid testimony to be the teachings of the greatest masters: Jesus, Buddha, Krishna, Moses, Abraham, Quetzalcoatl, Padmasambhava, Milarepa, the Dalai Lamas and all the types of teachers who are at the very pinnacle of development. Their teachings are what we consider valid testimony — teachers who fully exemplify what the teachings are guiding us to become. Thus, we are wary of those who are halfway, because they do not know everything, and easily make mistakes. We are very strict on that point.

There are many popular books, videos, theories, and teachings about spirituality. We are not interested in what is popular, modern, cutting edge. We are interested in the welfare of your very soul. Can you afford to take a risk on the teachings of someone who might be mistaken? In my opinion, we cannot. In my opinion, suffering is such a tremendous reality, and the potential for mistakes is so strong, that you have to be extraordinarily strict with yourself about what teachings you ingest, and believe, and follow, and act on. How can you gamble immortality, the chance to be liberated from suffering, on what is popular on the internet or in the bookstore? To me, that seems utterly ridiculous, foolish, and quite dangerous. Just because someone is skilled at selling books or making internet videos does not mean they know how to liberate you from suffering. Someone may be very charismatic, but that does not mean they are an awakened master who can help you as Krishna helps Arjuna.

Someone may have the best intentions in the world, but be completely wrong about what they teach others. That is why when it comes to our spiritual lives, we rely on Jesus,

Buddha, Moses, and other very high masters. That is what we consider valid testimony.

We need to analyze all of these things in ourselves on a daily basis. That is why we point them out.

The next three modifications are vikalpa, nidra, and smriti. These are Sanskrit words.

"Fantasy follows mere words that have no basis in reality.

"Sleep is a modification of mind based on abhava.

"Memory is not allowing impressions to escape." – *Yoga Sutras*

Fantasy (Vikalpa)

The scripture says that "fantasy follows mere words that have no basis in reality." This characterizes a huge percentage of the contents of our mind. An enormous majority of what is in our mind is absolute fantasy, and based on nothing. This includes all the TV shows and movies and celebrities and politics and all the things that we ingest from media. All of that is utter fantasy. I know we take it very seriously. We think that movies are very important, and celebrities and TV shows and sports are very important, but it is all lies, based on nothing. It has absolutely no importance in relation with the soul. It is a type of witchcraft, if you will, a type of black magic. It is a hypnotic influence. We watch these actors, movies, stories, and celebrities, and all they are doing is lying. They project themselves to be something that they are not. What is worse, we believe it and we imitate it. Have you noticed that when you watch something that really interests you, you start to imitate the actor, maybe in the way you stand, the way you talk, the way you dress, the words you use, or the way you look around? You think, "Maybe I am looking like that guy now." We all do that. It is a consequence of being hypnotized. We watch that band that is so cool and we start dressing like them, acting like them, thinking like them, and their music runs through our heads all the time. That is a form of hypnosis. That is fantasy.

We follow a particular fashion or a particular culture or a particular political movement or any type of theory or doctrine that wants us to affirm that we are a certain way, we are "born again," or we are "the chosen ones." All of that is fantasy, because not one atom of it can be confirmed by direct perception, not a single particle. It is all just words, beliefs, nothing. That is fantasy.

You can see that our culture is completely and utterly hypnotized by fantasy, because when we point it out, people get angry. They say, "that's my band, that's my political party, my religion, my show, my style. How dare you contradict that?" We think it is something sacred, but we do not realize that it is utterly and completely meaningless, like an image in a mirror. There is nothing there. But that is the nature of our culture now. It is wrong knowledge.

Only Look at the Facts

What are the facts of our spirituality? How do we get really practical with our spirituality? Obviously, we have to focus on ourselves. Spirituality is really about our relationship with everything else. It is about who we are, and what we are, and what that means. So, what are we? Who are we? This is where we start; we start looking at the facts, really taking things down to the simplest level. But somehow, the simple things are very profound.

We have a lot of beliefs about ourselves, thoughts about ourselves, and abstract concepts about ourselves, but we do not really know a lot of facts. I do not mean facts like "I was born in such and such a year and my

name is this and that," and "I am from this
country and that place and I have these types
of experiences." Those are not facts. Those
are memories. Memories are subjective; they
are not real. By facts I mean: what is
happening right now, what can you perceive
and confirm is true?

Now this becomes a profound question. The
first thing it requires factually is: who is
looking? Who is perceiving? Is it the body? Is
it the eyes? Is it the ears? Is it the skin? Who is
this? That is a very profound question, and
really it should be the origin of our religious
pursuit, of our spiritual interest, because that
question points exactly where our suffering or
happiness springs, where our problems or
solutions originate.

The fact is, we cannot answer the question
with facts, because we have not confirmed the
facts through our own experience. We have
beliefs about who we are, about how we
perceive. We believe we have a soul and that
soul is our true identity, yet that is not a fact;
the soul is a real thing that can be
experienced, but it is not experienced through
thoughts or belief. Many believe they are
angels on earth, or chosen people, blessed by
God for some great purpose — there is an
infinitude of beliefs about the "self" and what
in us perceives — but all the spiritual and

religious beliefs and theories contradict each other, which tells us immediately that they are all illusions. Facts can be confirmed and proven.

So, we have abstract ideas about ourselves, we have theoretical knowledge, we have a lot of things that we have been told. But, truly we have very few facts about ourselves. This is what we need to change. What are the facts of our perceptions? What can we perceive and confirm? This approach originates a different way of approaching religion.

To describe religious pursuits, some traditions use the phrase "self-realization." But that English phrase is not accurate. It comes from Sanskrit, and the Sanskrit words are atma-jnana. Atma means self, while yana means knowledge, with the same meaning as gnosis: it is knowledge acquired through experience. So atma-jnana actually means self-knowledge. How did people change it to self-realization, and how did that phrase lose all real meaning? People now think "self-realization" is something easy, like getting on a plane and flying high in the sky. They really believe that reading our full and complete development is something easy that happens by itself, without any effort or struggle, or —more importantly — any need to change themselves. How wrong they are!

What is knowledge of self (atma jnana)? Let
us begin here and now, and ask ourselves:
who is this self? Who am I? Who is this here?

If we are willing to be superficial and say,
"Well my name is this and that and I have this
skin color and I am from this place," that all is
very superficial, and it does not lead to any
understanding. That is not real knowledge.
That is just appearances. We need to go
deeper, and perceive the answer in facts. We
need to look into ourselves and question
ourselves: what is past the mask I wear? What
is deeper than my superficial appearance?
Where does the question itself originate?

So, right at the start, we are doing a kind of
introspection. Instead of looking outside and
trying to ask, "What is God? What is Buddha?
What is dharma?" We are looking inside,
"What am I? What is this perception? Why
does it change? What is mind? What is
emotion?"

These questions, when asked and watched
and perceived, lead to real knowledge, real
understanding. Yet, those questions, and the
answers, are not resolvable through the
intellect, through thoughts, or through beliefs.
They can only be answered through
perception, thus they must also be asked that
way. So: instead of thinking about this, begin

to look at it. Look at yourself, and everything you perceive, with this questioning perception. When you arrive to a new place, a new situation, you have a questioning perception, an "open mind," some might say, but we are not talking about mind really, we are talking about how one sees. Thus, we need to continually use a questioning perception, a way of seeing that is always looking at things as though they are totally new.

Our Point of View

Let's talk about the word impossible and how it relates to the consciousness.

I am sure you have heard quite often that nothing is impossible, but, in a practical way, never understood what that really means.

The word impossible is not a word denoting fact. It may seem like a fact, but it is a feeling based on the level of consciousness a person is at. I will explain further.

If we take the example of a marathon runner it might help us to better understand. The marathon runner must run 26.2 miles. To the average, untrained person, this might seem impossible. However, to the trained athlete, or a person who understands that with proper training and time, it is very possible. What is the difference between these two people? The only difference is that the one who does not think it possible is in a mental state or consciousness where he cannot see beyond. The other, who thinks it possible, is able to understand the change that his consciousness will go through with active effort. And practical work, which is gnosis, will change the mentality towards it.

Try to correlate this to everything else we are speaking of and it will make more sense to you.

Now, let's talk about miracles. The word miracle is an incorrect word, and one that would not be used by a person at the Noetic level of consciousness.

To the person at Eikasia, a miracle is anything fantastical in their imagination, that materializes. To the person in Pistis, a miracle is anything that their belief (with no factual basis) would support that seems out of the realm of reason. To the person at Dianoia, a miracle would be anything that happens that defies the scientific basis of thinking they have. To the Noetic thinker, there are no miracles. Everything is within his perception and they can see all the possibilities of everything.

So, you can clearly see how the level of consciousness of the person directly affects everything they view, how they view it, and their expectations of things.

CHAPTER 4

Sublimation of the Mind

S hould an instinct be denied its expression and all ideas connected with it be repressed into the subconscious, trouble will ensue. The lower reaches of a river can be emptied by the simple expedient of placing a dam across its channel, but this does not solve the problem of the surplus water, which gathers head behind the obstruction until it bursts its banks and makes a morass of the upper reaches. If it is necessary to deflect a river from its bed, then an alternative course must be provided, for the water continues to come down from the hills and must, by some means, be disposed of.

It is precisely this engineering problem that the psychotherapist has to deal with. We know that a large percentage of mental and nervous disorders are caused by the repression of the sexual instinct. This great instinct, in its mental and physical aspects, is so fundamental and so powerful that it cannot, with safety to the individual, be entirely repressed, nor with safety to society be given free rein, and we are on the horns of a dilemma, for social laws demand that it shall only be expressed under very limited conditions-those of legal marriage, and even then not to an unlimited extent; and nature demands that it shall be expressed as soon as the physical organs of its manifestation are sufficiently developed to function.

The average man solves this problem for himself by conniving at the maintenance of a pariah class of women whose very existence is socially ignored and is a fertile source of misery, disease, and crime; but for women, unless they are prepared permanently to join the pariah class, a social safety valve does not exist, and we find among them a much higher percentage than among men suffering from those nervous troubles that are due to a repression of the sexual instinct, and this also applies to men who, whether from idealism or fear of disease, do not avail themselves of a compromise.

This problem would prove as intractable in the future as it has in the past were it not that we now know that the law of transmutation of energy from one form to another is as true for psychology as it is for physics, and sex force can be utilized for other purposes than physical reproduction. This process of conversion is technically known as sublimation.

This is one of the most important discoveries of occult psychology, for it provides the solution to grave social problems that menace the fabric of civilization.

How, in actual practice, can this result be achieved?

First, by altering our entire attitude toward sex, and realizing that a problem is not solved by ignoring its existence. Secondly, by taking the sex problem out of the domain of the subconscious into the conscious mind and frankly facing it and acquiring dominion over it by the practice of thought control, transmuting our emotions instead of repressing them; and thirdly, by providing a channel of creative interest down which may flow the energies we wish to deflect from their primitive channel of manifestation.

The key to the whole problem lies in this, the life force flows to the point of interest. If the interest and attention are centered upon physical sensation, then the life force will flow, or attempt to flow, through the channel of the reproductive organs, or if denied manifestation, will keep up a constant irritation and stimulation; but if the interest be shifted to an emotional or mental level, then the life force will find an outlet in creative activity upon these levels and drain the pressure from the physical.

The mental and physical habits of a lifetime are not easily broken, but if the thoughts be patiently and persistently kept away from physical sensation and concentrated upon external interests, the law of mental and physical habit will come to our aid, and the life force will learn to flow through its new channel with safety to the individual and benefit to society.

The process of thought control must not be confused with the dissociation of ideas. In dissociation we are dishonest with ourselves, denying that certain qualities exist in our natures; the ideas connected with them are repressed into our subconsciousness, and it is the involuntary subconscious censor that holds them down; whereas in thought control we admit the primitive side of our natures and set to work to train it, and because we know that dwelling upon mental pictures of a sexual nature produces a physical reaction, we exclude these ideas from the consciousness; but in this case, the repression is not into the subconscious mind, but into the foreconscious, and it is one of the voluntary censors that enforces the command and remains under our control.

The distinction between repression and dissociation must be clearly borne in mind in all re-educational work. A certain amount of repression is unavoidable in a social life; for each individual sacrifices something of his personal desires for the sake of the benefits of cooperation with his fellows, and the energy thus sacrificed is turned to social purposes. Dissociation, however, is always a pathology, and should never be allowed to occur.

CHAPTER 5

The Dimensions

I n this chapter, we will discuss the dimensions of evolution. We will only concern ourselves with dimensions three through six, namely explaining dimensions four through six, because reaching the sixth dimension is the goal of human life.

The Third Dimension

The upper realm of Malkuth resides in the third dimension and it is part of Assiah[26], the world of Action.

The Fourth Dimension

Found in the World of Formation, Yesod[27] resides in the fourth dimension. The fourth dimension is known as the lower astral plane.

The study of the symbolism of Yesod reveals two apparently incongruous sets of symbols. Upon the one hand we have the conception

---

[26] In Qabalistic terms, this refers to the lowest of the four spiritual worlds, the final level in the creative process which includes the physical universe.
[27] A sphere on the Tree of Life, above Malkuth, in the world of formation.

of Yesod as the foundation of the universe, established in strength; this is indicated by the

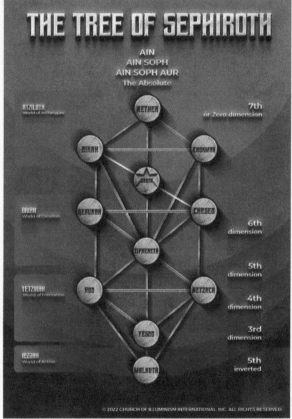

Figure 3 The Dimensions and the Tree of Life

recurrence of the idea of strength, as in the Magical Image of a beautiful naked man, very strong, the God-name of Shaddai,

Almighty, the Kerubim, the strong angels, and the Nine of Wands, whose secret name is the Lord of Great Strength. But upon the other hand we have the Moon symbolism, which is very fluidic, in a continual state of flux and reflux, under the presidency of Gabriel, the archangel of the element of Water.

How are we to reconcile these conflicting concepts? The answer is to be found in the words of the Yetziratic[28] Text, which says of the Ninth Path that it "purifies the Emanations. It proves and corrects the designing of their representations and disposes of the unity with which they are designed without diminution or division." This concept is further illuminated by the nature of the Spiritual Experience assigned to Yesod, which is described as "the Vision of the Machinery of the Universe."

We get the concept, then, of the fluidic waters of chaos being finally gathered up and organized by means of the "representations" that were "designed" in Hod; this final "proving, correcting, and disposing of the unity" of these "representations" or formative images resulting in the organization of the "Machinery of the Universe," the vision of

---

[28] Having relation to the Sefer Yetzirah, translated as the Bookf of Formation. It is the title of a book on Jewish mysticism.

which constitutes the spiritual experience of this Sephirah. In fact, Yesod might aptly be described as the Sphere of the Machinery of the Universe. If we liken the kingdom of earth to a great ship, then Yesod would be the engine-room.

Yesod is the sphere of that peculiar substance, partaking of the nature of both mind and matter, which is called the Ether of the Wise, the Akasha, or the Astral Light, according to the terminology that is being used. It is not the same as the ether of the physicists, which is the fire element of the Sphere of Malkuth; but is to that ether what that ether is to dense matter; it is, in fact, the basis of the phenomena which the physicist attributes to his empirical ether. The Ether of the Wise might, in fact, be called the root of the ether of physics.

The material universe is an insoluble riddle to the materialist because he insists on trying to explain it in terms of its own plane. This is a thing that can never be done in any sphere of thought. Nothing can ever be explained in terms of itself, but only by being resumed in a greater whole. The four elements of the ancients find their explanation in a fifth, the Ether, as initiates have always maintained. For it is a doctrine of esoteric philosophy that any four visible states always have their root in a fifth, an invisible state. For instance, the Four Worlds of the Qabalists have their root behind the Veils of the Unmanifest. It is only by positing this unmanifest fifth and assigning to it certain attributes deduced from the manifest four as being essential in the prime cause, that we are able to arrive at any understanding of the nature of the four. So do we find in Yesod the unmanifest fifth of the four elements of Malkuth, the fire of the ancients answering to the ether of the moderns, and earth, water, and air to the solid, liquid, and gaseous states of matter.

Yesod, then, must be conceived of as the receptacle of the emanations of all the other Sephiroth, as is taught by the Qabalists, and as the immediate and only transmitter of these emanations to Malkuth, the physical plane. As the Yetziratic Text says, it is the function of Yesod to purify the emanations, and to prove and correct them; consequently, it is in the Sphere of Yesod that all operations are carried out which are designed for the correcting of the Sphere of dense matter, or in any way to dispose of its unity of design. Yesod, then, is the all-important Sphere for any magic which is designed to take effect in the physical world.

Now be it well noted that all Spheres operate according to their nature, and that that nature cannot in any way be altered by any magical or miraculous influence, however powerful; we can only "correct" the "designing" of the representations. The things represented remain constant. The conditions of the material world cannot therefore be arbitrarily disposed of, even by the highest spiritual force, as is believed by those who pray to God to intervene on their behalf, healing their diseases or giving rain upon earth; neither can they any more be influenced by the most powerful wizard with his spells. The only approach to Malkuth is through Yesod, and the approach to Yesod is through Hod, where the "representations" are "designed." Let us once and for all disabuse our minds of the idea that spirit can work directly upon matter; it never does so. Spirit works through mind, and mind works through the 'Ether; and the 'Ether, which is the framework of matter and the vehicle of the life-forces, can be manipulated within the limits of its nature, which are by no means inconsiderable. All miraculous and supernatural happenings, therefore, are brought about by the manipulation of the natural qualities of the 'Ether, and if we understood the nature of the 'Ether, we should understand the rationale of their production. We should no longer attribute them to the direct intervention of

God, or to the activities of the spirits of the departed, than we attribute nowadays the phenomena of combustion to the activities of phlogiston, which a previous generation believed to be the active principle of fire, whose presence or absence determined whether a given substance would burn or not. There are men living to-day who learnt about phlogiston in their school-days, and have seen the change of thought come about; equally, the day will come when men will look upon psychic phenomena and "spiritual" healing as we look upon phlogiston.

The first of these properties is the capacity of the astral 'Ether to be molded into forms by the mind; the second is the capacity of the astral 'Ether to hold the molecules of dense matter in its mesh-like lines of tension as in a rack of pigeon-holes. It may be asked, how do we know that the ether possesses these qualities, so vital to our magical hypothesis? We answer that the existence of these properties is the only explanation of the properties of living matter and conscious mind. We cannot explain either mind or matter in terms of themselves alone; we cannot explain mind without employing terms of sensation, and we cannot explain living matter without employing terms of consciousness. Sensation must always be an affair of both mind and matter inexplicable in isolation. To explain neural sensation, we must posit a substance that is intermediate between mind and matter; to understand purposive movement we equally require the existence of such a substance-that is, which possesses the power to receive and hold the impress of thought and to influence the position in space of the atomic units of matter. These are the properties we assign to our hypothetical astral 'Ether', advancing the same arguments in justification of this proceeding as have been accepted on behalf of a similar proceeding in the case of the ether of physics. We plead for our hypothesis; and if the arguments in favor of the ether of physics are acceptable, it is difficult to see why an 'Ether' should not be permitted to psychology. It is an old maxim that hypotheses should not be unnecessarily multiplied, but when an hypothesis such as that of ether has proved so fruitful, we are surely amply justified in experimenting with a similar one in the sister science of psychology. One thing is quite certain, psychology never made any real progress while it limited itself to the materialistic viewpoint and regarded consciousness as an epiphenomenon, that is to say as, an irrelevant and purposeless by-product of physiological activity if anything in Nature can be called irrelevant and purposeless. Let us learn a lesson from coal-tar, the irrelevant and purposeless by-product of the production of gas-to be practically given away to anyone who wanted to tar a fence, subsequently found to be the source of most valuable chemicals, dye-stuffs, and drugs.

From the point of view of magic, Yesod is the all-important Sephirah[29], just as Tiphareth[30] is the functional sphere of mysticism, with its transcendent contacts with the Supernal. If the Tree of Life be considered as a whole, it will be seen clearly that it works in triads. The Three Supernals having their correlatives on a lower arc in Chesed[31], Geburah[32], and Tiphareth. Anyone who has had experience of practical Qabalism knows that for all practical purposes Tiphareth is Kether[33] for us while we tabernacle in this house of flesh, for no man may look upon the face of God and live. We can only see the Father reflected in the Son, and Tiphareth shows us the Father."

Netzach[34], Hod[35], and Yesod form the Lower Triad, overshadowed by Tiphareth as the Lower Self is overshadowed by the Higher

---

[29] Singular form of the word Sephiroth (sphere), referring to the Tree of Life.
[30] Hebrew; meaning Beauty; the sixth sephirah.
[31] Hebrew; meaning kindness or love between people; another sephirah.
[32] Hebrew; meaning strength; another sephirah.
[33] Hebrew; meaning crown; the topmost sephirah.
[34] Hebrew; meaning everlasting; the seventh sephirah.
[35] Hebrew; meaning splendor; the eighth sephirah.

Self. One might, in fact, say that the four lower Sephiroth form the Personality, or unit of Incarnation, of the Tree; the Higher Triad of Chesed, Geburah, and Tiphareth form the Individuality, or Higher Self, and the Three Supernals correspond to the Divine Spark.

It will be observed that although each Sephirah is considered to emanate its successor, the Triads are always represented, when once emanated and in equilibrium, as a Pair of Opposites manifesting in a Functional Third. In this, the Lower Triad, then, we find Netzach and Hod equilibrated in Yesod, which is conceived as receiving their emanations. But it also received the emanations of Tiphareth, and through Tiphareth, of Kether, because there is always a line of force working down a Pillar; consequently, as it received also from Netzach and Hod the influences that they in their turn have received from their respective Pillars, it may aptly be called, in the words of Qabalists, the "receptacle of the emanations"; and it is from Yesod that Malkuth receives the influx of the Divine forces.

Yesod also is of supreme importance to the practical occultist because it is the first Sphere with which he makes acquaintance when he commences to "rise on the planes," and lifts consciousness above Malkuth. Having

trodden the terrible Thirty-second Path of the
Tau or Cross of Suffering, and of Saturn, he
enters Yesod, the Treasure House of Images,
the sphere of Maya, Illusion. Yesod,
considered by itself, is unquestionably the
Sphere of Illusion, because the Treasure
House of Images is none other than the
Reflecting Aether of the Earth-sphere, and
corresponds in the microcosm to the
Unconscious of the psychologists, filled with
ancient and forgotten things, repressed since
the childhood of the race.

The Keys that unlock the doors of the
Treasure House of Images and enable us to
command its denizens are to be found in
Hod, the Sphere of Magic. It is truly said in
the Mysteries that no degree becomes
functional until one has taken the next.

Anyone who tries to function as a magician in
Yesod soon learns his error, for although he
can perceive the Images in the Treasure
House, he has no word of power with which
to command them. Therefore, in initiation
upon the Western Path, at any rate, the grades
of the Lesser Mysteries go straight up the
Central Pillar to Tiphareth, and do not follow
the line of the Lightning Flash. In Tiphareth
the initiate takes the first grade of adepthood,
and from there returns, if he so desires, to
learn the technique of the magician relative to

the Personality of the Tree, that is to say, the macrocosmic unit of incarnation. If he does not desire this but wishes to become free from the wheel of Birth and Death, he proceeds up the Central Pillar, which is also called by the Qabalists the Path of the Arrow, and passes over the Abyss into Kether. He who enters this Light cometh not forth again.

Yesod is also the Sphere of the Moon; therefore, to understand its significance we must know something about the way in which the Moon is regarded in occultism. It is held by initiates that the Moon separated from the Earth at the period when evolution was on the cusp between the etheric phase of its development and the phase of dense matter. Those who are familiar with the terminology of astrology will know that the cusp is that phase between two signs wherein the influence of both is intermingled. The Moon, then, has something of the material in its composition, hence the luminous globe we see in the sky; but the really important part of its composition is etheric, because it was during the phase of evolution when life was developing the etheric form that the Moon had its heyday, and for this reason the phase is called by some occultists the Luna Phase of evolution. Those who want to know more of this subject will find it dealt with in The

Rosicrucian[36] Cosmo-conception, by Max Heindel, and The Secret Doctrine, by Madame Blavatsky. As the Qabalists use a different system of classification to the Vedantists, we cannot open up the vast subject of the "Rays and the Rounds" in these pages. It must suffice to give dogmatically certain facts known to occultists and indicate where the reader can find further information if he desires it.

The Moon and the Earth, according to the occult theory, share one etheric double. Though their two physical bodies are separate, and the Moon is the senior partner; that is to say, in etheric matters the Moon is the Positive Pole of the battery, and the Earth the negative one. Yesod, as we have already seen, reflects the Sun of Tiphareth, which, in its turn, is Kether on a lower arc. Astronomers have long told us that the Moon shines by borrowed light, reflected from the Sun, and they are now beginning to hint that the Sun may receive its fiery energy from outer space. Translated into Qabalistic terminology, outer space would be the Great Unmanifest, and the Qabalists have taught this doctrine since the days when Enoch walked with God and was not, for God had taken him-in other

---

[36] Spiritual and cultural movement that arose in Europe in the early 17th century.

words, he had received the initiation of Kether.

It will be seen from the above that Yesod-Luna is ever in a state of flux and reflux, because the amount of sunlight received and reflected waxes and wanes in a twenty-eight-day cycle. Malkuth-Earth is also in a state of flux and reflux in a twenty-four-hour cycle, and for the same reason. Likewise, Malkuth-Earth has a three hundred and sixty-five day cycle, of which the phases are marked by the Equinoxes and the Solstices. It is the interacting set of these tides which is all-important to the practical occultist, because so much of his work depends upon them. The charts of these tides have always been kept secret, and some of them are exceedingly complex. As these concern the secret workings, the genuine and legitimate occult secrets, which are only given after initiation, they cannot be dealt with in these pages. Enough has been said, however, to indicate that certain tides in the lunar 'Ether' exist and are important, and that students of the occult are probably wasting their time if they try to operate without the necessary charts.

These lunar tides play a very important part in the physiological processes of both plants and animals, and especially in the germination and growth of plants and the reproduction of animals, as witness the twenty-eight-day lunar sexual cycle of the human female. The male has a sexual cycle based on the solar year, but in the artificially lit and heated houses of civilization this cycle is not so marked, though the poet drew our attention to the fact that "In the spring a young man's fancy lightly turns to thoughts of love," and the reference has been found so apt that it is almost too hackneyed for quotation.

It is the light of the Moon which is the stimulative factor in these etheric activities, and as Earth and Moon share one etheric double, all etheric activities are at their most active when the Moon is at its fullest. Likewise, during the dark of the Moon, etheric energy is at its lowest, and unorganized forces have a tendency to rise up and give trouble. The Dragon of the Qliphoth raises his multiple heads. In consequence, practical occult work is best let alone during the dark by all but experienced workers. The life-giving forces are relatively weak, and the unbalanced forces relatively strong; the result, in inexperienced hands, is chaos.

All psychics and sensitives are conscious of the set of these cosmic tides, and even those who are not avowedly sensitive are affected by them far more than is generally realized, especially in illness when the physical energies are low.

Not a great deal can be said concerning Yesod, because in her are hidden the keys of the magical workings. We must therefore content ourselves with elucidating the symbolism in a somewhat cryptic form, though he that hath ears to hear is at liberty to use them.

We have already noted the curious two-sided nature of Netzach and Hod, the magical image of Hod being a hermaphrodite, and Venus-Aphrodite sometimes being represented among the ancients as bearded. In Yesod, again, we meet with this dual symbolism, and yet again, as we shall see presently, in Malkuth. This indicates clearly that in these Sephiroth belonging to the lower levels of the Tree we must very definitely recognize a form and force side in each one. This comes out very clearly in both Yesod and Malkuth, to Which both gods and goddesses have to be assigned.

Yesod is essentially the Sphere of the Moon, and as such comes under the presidency of Diana, the moon-goddess of the Greeks. Now Diana was primarily a chaste goddess, ever-virgin, and when the over-presumptive Actaeon annoyed her, he was torn to pieces by his own hunting-hounds. Diana, however, was represented at Ephesus as the Many-breasted, and regarded as a fertility goddess. Moreover, Isis is also a lunar goddess, as indicated by the lunar crescent upon her brow, which in Hathor, becomes the cow-horns, the cow being among all peoples the especial symbol of maternity. In the Qabalistic symbolism, the generative organs are assigned to Yesod.

All this is very puzzling at first sight, for the symbols appear to be mutually exclusive. Carried a step further, however, we begin to find connecting links between the ideas.

The Moon has three goddesses assigned to her, Diana, Selene or Luna, and Hecate, the latter being the goddess of witchcraft and enchantments, and also presiding over child-birth.

There is also a very important moon-god, none other than Thoth himself, Lord of Magic. So then, when we find Hecate in Greece and Thoth in Egypt both assigned to the Moon, we cannot fail to recognize the importance of the Moon in matters magical. What then is the key to the magical Moon, who is sometimes a virgin goddess and sometimes a fertility goddess?

The answer is not very far to seek. It is to be found in the rhythmical nature of the Moon, and, in fact, in the rhythmical nature of sex-life in the female. There are times when Diana is many-breasted; there are times when her hounds tear the intruder to pieces.

In dealing with the rhythms of Luna we are dealing with etheric, not physical, conditions. The magnetism of living creatures waxes and wanes with a definite tide. It is a thing that is not difficult to observe when one knows what to look for. It shows itself most clearly in relations between persons in whom magnetism is fairly evenly balanced. Sometimes one will be in the ascendant, and sometimes the other.

Now, it may be asked, if the Sphere of Yesod is etheric, why are the generative organs assigned to this sphere, for surely their function is physical, if anything is? The answer to that question is to be found in the knowledge of the subtler aspects of sex which appears to be entirely lost to the Western world. It cannot be entered upon in detail in these pages, and it must suffice to point out that all the more important aspects of sex are etheric and magnetic. We might liken it to an iceberg, five-sixths of whose bulk is below the surface. The actual physical reactions of sex form a very small proportion, and by no means the most vital portion of its functioning. It is owing to our ignorance of this that so many marriages fail to fulfil the purpose of the welding of two halves into a perfect whole.

We take no account of the magical side of marriage, despite the fact that the Church classes it as a sacrament. Now a sacrament is defined as an outward and visible sign of an inward and spiritual grace, and it is that inward and spiritual grace which is so seldom found in the marriage act of the Anglo-Saxon races, with their relatively frigid temperament and contempt for the body. That inward and spiritual grace which makes of marriage a true sacrament after its kind is not the grace of sublimation, or renunciation, or a purity of denial and abstention; it is the grace of the blessing of Pan[37] in the joy in natural things so beautifully expressed by Walt Whitman in his poem-series, Children of Adam."

The assignation to Yesod of the perfumes and sandals is very significant. These two things play a very important part in magical operations. The sandals, or soft heelless Slippers that give free play to the foot, are always used in ceremonial work to tread the magical circle. They are as important a part of

---

37 From ancient Greek mythology; god of the wild.

the equipment of the practical occultist as his rod of power. God said unto Moses, "Put off thy shoes from off thy feet, for the place whereon thou standest is holy ground." The adept makes holy ground for himself by placing upon his feet the consecrated sandals. The floor-cloth, of the appropriate color and marked with the appropriate symbols, is also an important piece of lodge furniture. It is designed to concentrate the earth magnetism used in the Operation in the same way that the altar is the focus of the spiritual forces. Through our feet we pick up the earth magnetism; and when that magnetism is of a special kind, we use special slippers that shall not inhibit it.

The perfumes, too, are very important in ceremonial operations, for they represent the etheric side of the affair. Their psychological influence is well known, but the fine art of using them psychologically has been but little studied outside occult lodges. The use of perfumes is the most effectual way of playing on the emotions, and consequently of changing the focus of consciousness. How quickly do our thoughts turn away from earthly things when the drifting smoke of incense comes to us from the high altar; how quickly do they return to them again when we get a whiff of patchouli from the next pew!

And in the four Tarot cards assigned to this Sephirah how clearly do we see the workings of the etheric magnetism appearing. There is Great Strength when we are on the earth-contacts and blessed of Pan; there is also Material Happiness; in fact, without the blessing of Pan there can be no material happiness because there is no peace of the nerves. On its negative side, however, are to be found the depths of Despair and Cruelty; but with the earth-contacts firm under our feet there comes Material Gain because we are adequate to deal with the material plane.

The Fifth Dimension

Hod

The two root-powers of the universe are represented on the Tree of Life by Chokmah[38] and Binah[39], Positive and Negative Force. It is held by the Qabalists that although each Sephirah emanates its next in numerical order, that these two Supernals of the Tree being once established, are reflected down it diagonally in a particular way. This is clearly indicated in the Yetziratic Text of this Sephirah, wherein it says that Hod "has no root by which it can cleave or rest, save in the

---

[38] Hebrew; meaning wisdom; another sephirah.
[39] Hebrew; meaning understanding; the third sephirah.

hidden places of Gedulah[40], from whence emanates its proper essence". Gedulah, be it remembered, is another name for Chesed.

Binah is the Giver of Form. Chesed is cosmic anabolism, the organization of the units formulated by Binah into complex, interacting structures; Hod, the reflection of Chesed, is in its turn a Sephirah of Form, and represents this coagulating principle in another sphere.

Chokmah, on the other hand, is the dynamic principle; it reflects into Geburah, which is the Cosmic Katabolist, representing the breaking-down of the complex into the simple, thus releasing latent energy; and this reflects again into Netzach, the life-force of Nature.

It is important for the understanding of the five lower Sephiroth to note that the present stage of evolution has brought some degree of development of human consciousness in their Spheres. Tiphareth represents the higher consciousness wherein the individuality unites with the personality: Netzach and Hod represent the force and form aspects of astral consciousness respectively. Because human consciousness has made a degree of development in these spheres, their purely

---

[40] Hebrew; meaning greatness, magnificence, or glory.

cosmic nature is considerably overlaid by its influences; and as human consciousness, being developed in Malkuth, is a consciousness of forms derived from the experience of physical sensations, the conditions of Malkuth are reflected back, though in a rarefied form, into Hod and Netzach, and in a lesser degree into Tiphareth; Yesod is even more markedly conditioned by the rising influence of Malkuth.

This is due to the fact that the mind of any being of a sufficient degree of development to have achieved an independent will works objectively on its environment, thereby modifying it. Let us make this clear by an illustration. Creatures of a lowly development, such as the simple forms of life that have no motile power, like sea-anemones, can exercise very little influence over their environment; but a higher and more intelligent type of creature can exercise a great deal, forcing its environment, by its energy and intelligence, to conform to its will, as when a beaver builds a dam. Human beings, the highest of all the creatures of matter, have learnt to exercise a profound influence on their environment, so that the material globe is gradually being brought into subjection to man, whole spheres, in fact, being thus harnessed.

The conditions with regard to each level of consciousness are precisely analogous. The mind builds up out of mind-stuff and the spiritual nature out of the spiritual forces of the Cosmos in exactly the same way that the sea-anemone builds up its substance out of the nutriment brought to it by the water. The higher types of personality, however, are analogous to the higher types of animals in that they can in an increasing degree, according to their energy and capacity, influence their subtle environment; the mind, built up out of mind-stuff, making its influence felt in the plane of mind.

We observe in dealing with the astral plane, which is essentially the level of function of the denser aspects of the human mind, that the forces and factors of this plane present to consciousness as ethereal forms of a distinctly human type; and if we approach the subject philosophically, and not credulously, we are at a loss to explain how this can be. The initiate, however, has his explanation. He declares that it is the human mind itself which has created these forms by representing these intelligent natural forces to itself as having forms of a human type; reasoning by analogy that, because they are individualized, their individuality must have the same kind of vehicle for its manifestation as his own individuality.

This, of course, does not necessarily follow. In fact, these forms of life, left to their own devices, achieve incarnation in natural phenomena, their vehicles being co-ordinations of natural forces such as a river, a range of mountains, or a storm. Wherever man comes in touch with the astral, whether as psychic or magician, he always anthropomorphizes and creates forms in his own likeness to represent to himself the elusive subtle forces that he is endeavoring to contact, understand, and harness to his will. He is a true child of the Great Mother, Binah, and carries his natural propensities for organism and form-making to whatever plane he is able to exalt consciousness.

The forms perceived on the astral plane by those who can see there, are the forms that have been made by the imagination of men to represent these subtle natural forces of other forms of evolution than the human. The intelligences of other forms of evolution than ours, if they come into touch with human life, can sometimes be persuaded to make use of these forms, just as a man puts on a diving-suit and descends into another element. A certain, and fundamental, type of magic deals with the making of these forms and the inducing of entities to ensoul them.

Let us consider what is done when such a
process is afoot. Primitive man, who is much
more psychic than civilized man, his mind not
being so elaborately organized by education, is
intuitively aware that there is a subtle
something behind any highly organized unit
of natural force that differentiates it from
every other unit. Humans are subconsciously
aware of this to a greater degree than they will
admit; it is not for nothing that a ship is "she,"
and that we speak of "Father Thames." A
savage, then, feeling this life behind
phenomena, tries to get into touch with it in
order that he may come to terms with it. As
he obviously cannot hope to conquer it, he
must make terms with it, just as he would
with other alien lives ensouled in the bodies
of another tribe. In order to come to terms
there must be a parley. One cannot make
terms with persons who will not parley. The
savage thinks, reasoning by his own primitive
method of analogy, that the beings behind the
phenomena dwell in a kingdom similar to that
in which his own dream-life goes on; as
daydreams are close akin to the dreams of
sleep, and have the advantage of being
inducible at will, he tries to approach these
beings of another sphere by entering their
kingdom; that is to say, he fabricates in day-
dream or phantasy the closest approach he
can to the visions of the night, and if he can
achieve a high degree of concentration, he is

able to close down his waking consciousness and enter voluntarily into the dream state in a dream of his own determining.

In order to achieve this end, he builds up in his imagination a mental picture intended to represent the being that is the presiding genius of the natural phenomenon he wishes to come to terms with; he builds it up repeatedly; he adores it; he prays to it; he invokes it. If his invocation be sufficiently fervent, the being he is seeking will hear him telepathically and may become interested in what he is doing; if his adoration and sacrifices are agreeable to it, its co-operation may be obtained. Gradually it may become tamed and domesticated; and finally, it may be persuaded to ensoul from time to time the form that has been built up out of mind-stuff for its vehicle. Success in this operation depends, of course, on the degree to which the worshipper can appreciate through sympathy the nature of the being he is bent upon invoking, and he can only do this in proportion as his own temperament partakes of its nature.

If this process is successful, then we have the domestication of a portion of the life of Nature, and its incarnation in a form built for it by its worshippers. As long as the astral form is kept alive by the appropriate kind of worship, carried Out by worshippers who have the necessary capacity to enter into sympathetic communion with that kind of life, there is an incarnated god, available for contacting, brought down within the range of human perception. Should the worship cease, the god withdraws to his own place in the bosom of Nature. Should other worshippers come along, however, who possess the knowledge necessary to build a form in accordance with the nature of the life that is to be invoked, and the imaginative sympathy necessary to invoke it, it is a comparatively simple matter to attract into the form once more the life that was accustomed to ensoul it; no more difficult, at least, than to catch with a basket of oats a horse that has run wild on the ranges.

Now, it may be said, all this is the wildest speculation and sheer dogmatism. How do I know that that is the way in which primitive man went to work? Because that is the way of going to work that has come down in the secret Mystery Tradition from very ancient times, and because when it is used by anyone who has acquired the necessary degree of skill in concentration and knows the symbols that are used for building the different forms, the method works, and back come the Old Gods to the altar fires re-kindled. Definite results are obtained in the consciousness of the worshippers; and if they borrow the technique of the spiritualist, and a materializing medium is available, phenomena of a very definite kind are produced.

It is the method that is used in working the Mass by those priests who have knowledge. There are two types of priests in the Roman Church: the beneficed parish clergy and the men who belong to monastic Orders and undertake parish, and especially home mission, work as part of their service. These monks frequently bring to the working of the Mass a very high degree of magical power, as any psychic can testify. It is the ensouling of an astral form with spiritual force which is the real act of Transubstantiation. It is in the knowledge of these things, and in the possession of organized bodies of men and women trained in their use in the cloistered Orders, that the strength of the One Catholic and Apostolic Church lies; it is the lack of any such inner knowledge which is the weakness of the schismatic communions, a lack that makes the Anglican rituals, even when worked with full ceremonial, as water unto wine when compared with the Roman rituals; for the men who work them have no knowledge of the secret workings which are traditional in the Roman communion, and are not trained in the technique of visualizing. I am not a Catholic, and never shall be, because I would not submit to their discipline, nor do I believe that there is only One Name under heaven whereby men may be saved, much as I revere that Name, but I know power when I see it, and I respect it.

But the power of the Roman Church does not lie in charter, but in function. It is powerful, not because Peter received the Keys (which he probably didn't), but because it knows its job. There is no reason why priests of the Anglican communion should not work with power if they apply the principles I have explained in these pages. In the Guild of the Master Jesus, we work the Mass with Power because we apply these principles. When we first started we were offered Apostolic Succession for out ministrants, but declined it because we felt that it was better to use our knowledge to make the contacts anew on our own account than to receive Apostolic Succession from a source that was not above suspicion, and experience has justified our choice.

For the full understanding of the philosophy of magic we must remember that single Sephiroth are never functional; for function one must have the Pair of Opposites in balanced equilibrium, resulting in an equilibrated Third which is functional. The Pair of Opposites, by themselves, are not functional because they are mutually neutralizing; it is only when they unite in balanced force to flow forth as a Third, after the symbolism of Father, Mother, and Child, that they achieve dynamic activity, as distinguished from the latent force which is forever locked up in them, awaiting to be called forth.

The functioning triangle of the Lower Triad consists of Hod, Netzach, and Yesod. Hod and Netzach, as we have noted before, are respectively Form and Force on the astral plane. Yesod is the basis of etheric substance, Akasha, or the Astral Light, as it is variously called. Hod is especially the Sphere of Magic, because it is the sphere of the formulation of forms and is therefore the sphere in which the magician actually works, for it is his mind that formulates the forms, and his will that makes the link with the natural forces of the Sphere of Netzach that ensoul them. Be it noted, however, that without the contacts of Netzach, the force aspect of the astral, there could be no ensouling; and with Netzach, being the Sphere of emotions, the contacts are made through sympathy and "feeling with." The power of the will projects the magician out of Hod, but only the power of sympathy can take him into Netzach. A cold-blooded person of dominating will can no more be an adept working with power than can a fluidically sympathetic person of pure emotion. The power of the concentrated will is necessary to enable the magician to gather himself together for his work, but the power of imaginative sympathy is essential to enable him to make his contacts. For it is only through our power to enter imaginatively into the life of types of existence different to our own that we can pick up our contacts with the forces of Nature. To attempt to dominate them by pure will, cursing them by the Mighty Names of God if they resist, is sheer sorcery. As we have already noted, it is through the corresponding factors in our own temperaments that we come into touch with the forces of Nature. It is the Venus within that puts us in touch with the influences symbolized by Netzach. It is the magical capacity of our own mind that puts us in touch with the forces of the Sphere of Hod-Mercury- Thoth. If there is no Venus in our own nature, no capacity to respond to the call of love, the gates of the Sphere of Netzach will never open to us and we shall never receive its initiation. Equally, if we have no magical capacity, which is the work of the intellectual imagination, the Sphere of Hod will be a closed book to us. We can only operate in a Sphere after we have received the initiation of that Sphere, which, in the language of the Mysteries, confers its powers. In the technical working of the Mysteries these initiations are conferred on the physical plane by means of ceremonial, which may be effectual, or may not. The gist of the matter lies in the fact that one cannot waken into activity what is not already latent. Life is the real initiator; the experiences of life stimulate into function the capacities of our temperaments in such degree as we possess them. The ceremony of initiation, and the teachings that should be given in the various grades, are simply designed to make conscious what was previously subconscious, and to bring under the control of the will, directed by the higher intelligence, those developed reaction-capacities which have hitherto only responded blindly to their appropriate Stimuli.

Be it well noted that it is only in proportion as our capacities for reaction are lifted out of the sphere of emotional reflexes and brought under rational control that we can make of them magical powers. It is only when the aspirant, having the capacity to respond on all planes to the call of Venus, can easily and without effort refrain at will from responding, that he can be made an initiate of the Sphere of Netzach. This is why it is said of the adept that he has the use of all things, but is dependent upon nothing.

These concepts are shadowed forth for those who have eyes to see in the symbolism of Hod. The Yetziratic Text declares that Hod is the Perfect Intelligence because it is the mean of the Primordial. In other words, it is power in equilibrium, for the word "mean" implies a position half-way between two extremes.

The concept of inhibited reaction and satisfaction foregone is expressed in the title of the Eight of Cups of the Tarot pack, whose secret name is" Abandoned Success." The suit of Cups, in the Tarot symbolism, is under the influence of Venus and represents the different aspects and influences of love. "Abandoned Success," the inhibition of the instinctive reaction which would give satisfaction-in other words, sublimation-is the key to the powers of Hod. But remember that sublimation is not the same thing as either repression or eradication, and it applies to the instinct of self-preservation as well as to the instinct of reproduction, with which it is exclusively associated in the popular mind.

The same concept reappears in the secret title of the Eight of Swords, which is "The Lord of Shortened Force." We get a clear image in these words of the checking, or braking of dynamic power in order that it may be brought under control.

In the Eight of Pentacles, which represents the nature of Hod manifesting on the material plane, we have the Lord of Prudence-again a checking and inhibiting influence. But all these three negative, inhibiting cards are summed up under the presidency of the Eight of Wands, which represents the action of the Sphere of Hod on the spiritual plane, and this card is called the Lord of Swiftness.

We see, then, that it is through inhibitions and refraining on the lower planes that the dynamic energy of the highest plane is rendered available. It is in the Sphere of Hod that the rational mind imposes these inhibitions on the dynamic animal nature of the soul; condensing them; formulating them; directing them by limiting them and preventing diffusion. This is the operation of the magic that works with symbols. By its means, the free-moving natural forces are constrained and directed to ends that are willed and designed. This power of direction and control is only obtained by the sacrifice of fluidity, and Hod is therefore aptly said to be the reflection of Binah through Chesed. Having considered the general principles of the Sphere of Hod, we are now in a position to consider its symbolism in detail.

The meaning of the Hebrew word Hod is Glory, and this suggests at once to the mind that in this, the first Sphere in which forms are definitely organized, the radiance of the Primordial is shown forth to human consciousness. Physicists tell us that light is only rendered visible as blue sky owing to its reflection from the particles of dust in the atmosphere. Absolutely dustless atmosphere is absolutely dark atmosphere. And so it is in the metaphysics of the Tree. The glory of God can only shine forth in manifestation when there are forms to manifest it.

The Magical Image of Hod affords a very interesting subject for meditation. Those who have grasped the significance of the preceding pages will see how well the form- and-force nature of magical working is summed up in this symbol of the being in whom are combined the male and female elements.

Hod is essentially the sphere of forms ensouled by the forces of Nature; and conversely, it is the sphere in which the forces of Nature take on sensible form.

The Yetziratic Text has already been discussed at length, and to that discussion the reader can refer for its elucidation.

The God-name of Hod, Elohim Tzabaoth, God of Hosts, contains the hermaphroditic symbol in a very interesting way, for the word Elohim is a feminine noun with a masculine plural, thus indicating in the manner of the Qabalists that it represents a dual type of activity, or force functioning through an organization. All three Sephiroth in the Negative Pillar of the Tree have the word Elohim as part of the God name. Tetragrammaton Elohim in Binah; Elohim Gebor in Geburah; and Elohim Tzabaoth in Hod.

The word Tzabaoth means a host or army, and so we get the idea of the Divine Life manifesting in Hod by means of a host of forms ensouled with force, in contradistinction to the fluidic activity of Netzach.

The assignation of the mighty Archangel Michael to Hod again gives us food for thought. He is always represented as trampling upon a serpent and piercing it with a sword, and frequently holds in his hand a pair of balances, symbolic of equilibrium and expressive of the same idea as the Yetziratic words, "Mean of the Primordial."

The serpent upon which the great Archangel treads is primitive force, the phallic serpent of the Freudians; and this glyph teaches us that it is the restrictive "prudence" of Hod which "shortens" primitive force and prevents it from overflowing its boundaries. The Fall, be it remembered, is represented on the Tree by the Great Serpent with seven heads which overpasses the bounds set for it and raises its crowned heads even unto Daath. It is very interesting to observe the manner in which the symbols weave in and out of each other, and reinforce and interpret each other's significance and yield their fruits to Qabalistic contemplation.

The Order of Angels functioning in Hod are the Beni Elohim, the Sons of the Gods. Again, we have the concept of the "God of Hosts" or armies. One of the most important concepts of arcane science concerns the working of the Creator through intermediaries. The uninitiated and profane conceive of God as working as the laborer works, who adds brick to brick with his hands, fashioning the edifice; but the initiated conceive of God as working as the Great Architect of the Universe, designing His plans on the plane of archetypes; to Whom come the overseers, the archangels, for their instructions, these last directing the armies of humble toilers who add stone to stone according to the archetypal plan of the Most High. Whenever did the architect designing the edifice work upon it with his two unaided hands? Never, not even when the universe was building.

The Mundane Chakra, as we have already noted, is Mercury, and its symbolism as Hermes-Thoth we have already considered.

The Spiritual Experience assigned to this Sephirah is the Vision of Splendor, which is the realization of the glory of God manifesting in the created world. The initiate of Hod sees behind the appearance of created things and discerns their Creator, and in the realization of the splendor of Nature as the garment of the Ineffable, he receives his illumination and becomes a co-worker with the Great Artificer. It is this realization of the spiritual forces manipulating all manifestations and appearances which is the key to the powers of Hod as wielded in the Magic of Light. It is by making himself a channel for these forces that the Master of White Magic brings order into the disorder of the Spheres of Unbalanced Force, not by deflecting the invisible powers to his personal will. He is the equilibrator of the unbalanced, not the arbitrary manipulator of Nature.

In this Sphere, which is the Sphere of Mercury-Hermes, god of science and books, how clearly can we see that the supreme virtue is truthfulness, and that the obverse aspect of this Sephirah is that which reveals Mercury in his aspect as the god of thieves and cunning rogues. In esoteric ethics it is realized that

102

each plane has its own standard of right and wrong. The standard of the physical plane is strength; the standard of the astral plane is beauty; the standard of the mental plane is truth; and the standard of the spiritual plane is that of right and wrong as we understand the terms; therefore, there is no ethic except in terms of spiritual value; all else is at best expediency. In the Sphere which is essentially the Sphere of the concrete mind, how right it is that the Qabalah should give the supreme virtue as truthfulness.

The Correspondence in the Microcosm is given as the loins and legs, in accordance with the astrological ruling of the planet Mercury.

The symbols associated with Hod are given as the names and versicles and the apron. The names are the Words of Power wherein the magus sums up and evokes into consciousness the multiform potencies of the Beni Elohim. These names are by no manner of means arbitrary and barbaric vocables, without etymology or meaning. They are philosophical formulae. In some cases, their interpretation is etymological, as in the case of the Egyptian deities, whose names are built up out of the names of potencies and symbols when used to indicate composite forces. In all systems of magic, however, which have their root in the Qabalah, the magical names are

built up out of the numerical value of the
consonants of whatever sacred alphabet is
used; there is a Greek, an Arabic, and a Coptic
Qabalah, as well as the better-known Hebrew
one. These consonants, when replaced by the
appropriate numerals, yield a number, which
can be dealt with mathematically in many
ways. Some of these ways are according to the
methods of pure mathematics, the results
being then translated back into letters again,
and showing very interesting correspondences
with the names of similar or related potencies.
This is a very curious aspect of Qabalistic lore,
and in the hands of competent exponents
yields interesting results; it is, however, full of
pitfalls for the unwary, for there is no limit to
what it can be made to yield, and only a sound
knowledge of first principles can tell us when
the analogies are legitimate or otherwise, and
prevent us from falling into credulity and
superstition.

The versicles are mantric phrases, a mantra
being a sonorous phrase which, when
repeated over and over after the manner of a
rosary, works upon the mind as a special form
of auto-suggestion, the psychology of which is
too complex to be entered upon now.

The apron has immediate associations for the
initiates of Solomon the Wise; it is the
characteristic garment of the initiate in the

Lesser Mysteries, who is always deemed figuratively to be a craftsman, that is a maker of forms, and as the Sephirah Hod is the Sphere of the operations of the makers of magical forms, it will be seen that this symbolism is again apposite. The apron covers and conceals the Moon-center, Yesod, concerning which we shall speak in its appropriate place. As has already been noted, Yesod is the functional aspect of the Pair of Opposites of the astral plane.

Concerning the four Eights of the Tarot pack, assigned to this Sephirah, we have already spoken on a previous page.

To sum up, then, in Hod we have the Sphere of formal magic as distinguished from simple mind power. The forms that are formulated thereon by the magician initiating the forces of nature are the Beni Elohim, or Sons of the Gods.

Netzach

Netzach, the Sphere of Venus, is best understood by contrasting it with Hod, the Sphere of Mercury, these two representing force and form on a lower arc, as has already been seen. Netzach represents the instincts and the emotions they give rise to, and Hod represents the concrete mind. In the macrocosm they represent two levels of the process of the concretion of force into form. In Netzach, force is still relatively free-moving, being bound only into exceedingly fluidic and ever-shifting shapes, and in Hod, taking on for the first time definite and permanent form, though of an exceedingly tenuous nature. In Netzach, a particular form of force represents itself as a type of beings, flowing backwards and forwards over the boundaries of manifestation in an exceedingly elusive manner. Such beings have no individualized personalities but are like the armies with banners that can be seen in the sunset clouds. In Hod, however, individualization into units has taken place, and there is continuity of existence. All mind is group-mind in Netzach, but in Hod the human mind has its beginnings.

Let us now consider Netzach itself, both in its microcosmic and macrocosmic aspects, bearing constantly in mind that we are now in the sphere of illusion, and that what is about to be described in terms of form are appearances as represented by the intellect to itself and projected back into the astral light as thought-forms. This is a very important point and should be thoroughly understood in order to avoid falling into superstition. Everything that is perceived by the "eyes of the intellect and the contemplations of faith," as the

Yetziratic Text so graphically puts it, has its
metaphysical basis in Chokmah, the Supernal
Sephirah at the head of the Pillar of Mercy.
But with Netzach a great change comes over
our mode of apprehending the different types
of existence assigned to each sphere. Hitherto
we have perceived by means of intuition; our
apprehensions have been formless, or at least
represented by highly abstract symbols; there
are no more of these after Tiphareth, but we
come to such concrete symbols as the rose,
assigned to Venus, for Netzach, and the
caduceus, assigned to Mercury, for Hod.

As has been seen, we conceive of the higher
Sephiroth under the aspect of factors of
manifestation and functions. We will see in
our study of Tiphareth how the Mediating
Intelligence, as the Sepher Yetzirah calls it,
broke up the White Light of the One Life as
in a prism so that it becomes the Refulgent
Splendor of many-rayed hues in Netzach.
Here we have not force, but forces; not life,
but lives. Appropriately, therefore, the Order
of Angels assigned to Netzach are the
Elohim, or gods. The One has been reduced
to the Many for the purposes of manifestation
in form.

These rays are not represented as the pure
white light by which we see everything in its
true colors, but as many-hued, each one of

which brings out and intensifies some specialized aspect of manifestation, just as a ray of blue light will only show up those colors that are sympathetic to it and will make its complementary colors look black. Every life or form of force manifesting in Netzach is a partial but specialized manifestation; therefore, no being that has for its sphere of evolution the sphere of Netzach can ever have an all-round development, but must always be a creature of one idea, one single, simple, stereotyped function.

It is the Netzach factor in ourselves that is the basis of our instincts, each of which, in their unintellectualized essence, gives rises to appropriate reflexes. The beings of Netzach, the Elohim, are not so much intelligences as the embodiments of ideas.

These Elohim, to give them their Hebrew name, are the formative influences whereby the creative force expresses itself in Nature. Their true character is to be discerned in Chesed, where they are described by the Sepher Yetzirah as the "Holy Powers". In Netzach, however, which represents the upper stratum of the reflecting ether, they undergo a change, the image-making mind of man has begun to work upon them, molding the astral light into forms that shall represent them to his consciousness.

It is very important that we should realize that these lower Sephiroth of the Plane of Illusion are densely populated by thought-forms; that everything which the human imagination has been able to conceive, however dimly, has a form built about it out of the astral light, and that the more the human imagination has dwelt upon it to idealize it, the more definite that form becomes. Consequently, subsequent generations of seers, when they seek to discern the spiritual nature and inner most essence of any form of life, are met by these images, the "creations of the created", and will be deceived thereby, mistaking them for the abstract essence itself, which is not to be found upon any plane that yields images to psychic vision, but only upon those that are discerned by pure intuition.

When his mentality was still primitive man worshipped these images, by means of which he represented to himself the great natural forces so all-important to his material well-being, thus establishing a link with them, by means of which a channel was developed whereby the forces they represented were poured into his soul, thus stimulating the corresponding factor in his own nature and thereby developing it. The operations of this worship, especially when it became highly organized and intellectualized, as in Greece and Egypt, built up exceedingly definite and potent images, and it is these that are generally understood as the gods. Generations of worship and adoration build a very strong image in the astral light, and when sacrifice is added to worship, the image is brought a step farther down the planes into manifestation and acquires a form in the dense ethers of Yesod, and is a very potent magical object, capable of independent action when ensouled by the concrete ideas generated in Hod.

We see, then, that every celestial being conceived by the mind of man has as its basis a natural force, but that upon the basis of this natural force is built up a symbolic image representative thereof, which is ensouled and rendered active by the force it represents. The image, then, is but a mode of representation indulged in by the human mind for its own convenience, but the force that the image represents, and which ensouls it, is a very real thing indeed, and under certain circumstances can be exceedingly powerful. In other words, although the form under which the god is represented is pure imagination, the force associated with it is both real and active.

This fact is the key, not only to talismanic magic in its broadest sense, which includes all consecrated objects used in ceremonial work and for meditation, but to many things in life that we cannot fail to observe, but for which we have no explanation. It explains a great many things in organized religion that are very real to the believer but very baffling to the unbeliever, who can neither explain them nor explain them away.

In Netzach, however, we have the most tenuous form of these things, and they are perceived far more by the "contemplations of faith" than by the "eyes of the intellect." In the Sphere of Hod are performed all manner of magical operations in which the intellect itself is brought to bear upon these tenuous and fleeting images to give them form and permanency; but in the Sphere of Netzach, such operations do not take place to any great degree; all god-forms in Netzach are worshipped by means of the arts, not conceived by means of philosophies.

Nevertheless, for all practical purposes it is impossible to separate the activities of Hod and Netzach, which are a functional pair, just as Geburah and Chesed make up the two aspects of metabolism, the katabolic and the anabolic. The functions of Netzach are implicit in Hod because Netzach emanates Hod, and the powers developed by evolution in the Sphere of Netzach are the basis of the capacities of Hod. Consequently, all magical operations of the Sphere of Hod work upon a basis of the tenuous life-forms of Netzach;

and because the human intellect works up from Sphere to Sphere, a good deal of the powers of Hod have been carried over into Netzach by initiated souls going on ahead of evolution. The two Spheres, therefore, are not clear-cut in their division and classification, but in each one a certain type of function very definitely predominates.

The contacts of Netzach are not made by means of conceiving its life philosophically, nor by means of ordinary image-making psychism, but by "feeling with," as Algernon Blackwood has so graphically expressed it in his novels, into which so much of the Sphere of Netzach enters. It is by means of dance and sound and color that the Netzach angels are contacted and evoked. The worshipper of a god in the Sphere of Netzach enters into communion with the object of his adoration by means of the arts; and in proportion as he is an artist in some medium or other, and can therein represent his deity symbolically, will he be able to make the contact and draw the life into himself. All rites which have rhythm and movement and color in them, are a working in the Sphere of Netzach. And as Hod, the Sphere of magical workings, draws its force from Netzach, it follows that any magical operation of the Sphere of Hod must have a Netzach element in it if it is to be ensouled effectually; and in order to provide a basis of manifestation, etheric substance has to be provided by some form of sacrifice, even if it be only the burning of incense. This question will be dealt with fully in studying the Sphere of Yesod, to which it belongs. It is necessary to refer to it here, because the significance of the rites of Netzach cannot be understood without a realization of the means whereby manifestation is effected, and the god brought near to his worshippers.

Let us now consider Netzach from the point of view of the microcosmic Tree of Life- that is to say, the subjective Tree within the soul, wherein the Sephiroth are factors in consciousness.

The Three Supernals, and the first pair of manifesting Sephiroth, Chesed and Geburah, represent the Higher Self, with Tiphareth as the point of contact with the Lower Self. The four lower Sephiroth, Netzach, Hod, Yesod, and Malkuth, represent the Lower Self, or personality, the unit of incarnation, with Tiphareth as the point of contact with the Higher Self, which is sometimes called the Holy Guardian Angel[41].

---

[41] The transcendent spiritual self that mediates between the Divine Self and the Lower Personality. Used by Abramelin the Mage.

From the point of view of the personality,
Tiphareth represents the higher
consciousness, aware of spiritual things;
Netzach represents the instincts, and Hod the
intellect. Yesod represents the fifth element,
Kether, and Malkuth the four elements which
are the subtle aspect of matter. All that the
average human intellect can realize is the
nature of dense matter, Malkuth, and of the
intellect, Hod, both concrete aspects of
existence. It has no appreciation of the forces
which build the forms, as represented by
Netzach, the Sphere of the instincts, and
Yesod, the etheric double or subtle body.
Consequently, we must make a careful study
of Netzach because its nature and importance
are so little understood.

We shall comprehend the nature of Netzach
in the microcosm best if we remember that it
is the Sphere of Venus, with all that that
implies. Translated from the symbolic
language of the Qabalah into plain English, it
means that we are concerned here with the
function of polarity, which is a very great deal
more than mere sex as popularly conceived.
It is important to note in this respect that
Venus, or in her Greek form, Aphrodite, is
not a fertility goddess at all, such as are Ceres
and Persephone; she is the goddess of love.
Now in the Greek concept of life, love
embraced much more than the relationship

between the sexes. It included the comradeship of fighting men and the relationship of teacher and pupil. The Greek hetaira, or woman whose profession is love, was something very different to our modern prostitute. The Greek kept the simple physical relation of the sexes for his lawful wife, who was secluded in the gynoecium, or harem, and was kept simply for breeding purposes in order that he might have lawful heirs; and she was a woman without education, though of good blood, and was not encouraged to render herself attractive, or play the arts of love. Still less was she encouraged to worship the goddess Aphrodite, who presides over the higher aspects of love; the deities of her adoration were expected to be the gods of hearth and home; Ceres, the earth-mother, was the ruler of the Mysteries of the Greek women.

The Aphrodite cult was something very much more than the simple performance of an animal function. It was concerned with the subtle interaction of the life-force between two factors; the curious flow and return, the stimulus and the reaction, which plays so important a part in the relations of the sexes but extends far beyond the sphere of sex.

The Greek hetaira was expected to be a woman of culture; there were, of course, all grades among them, the lower, who approximated to the Japanese geisha, to the higher, who held salons after the manner of the famous French blue-stockings, and were women of clean physical virtue to whom no man would dare to make sensual advances; but because of the reverence in which the function of sex was held among the Greeks, it is probable that at no grade of society did the hetaira approximate to the degradation of the modern professional prostitute.

The function of the hetaira was to minister to the intellect of her clients as well as their appetites; she was a hostess as well as a mistress, and to her resorted the philosophers and poets to receive inspiration and sharpen their wits; for it was well realized that there is no greater inspiration to an intellectual man than the society of a vital and cultured woman.

In the temples of Aphrodite, the art of love was sedulously cultivated, and the priestesses were trained from childhood in its skill. But this art was not simply that of provoking passion, but of adequately satisfying it on all levels of consciousness; not simply by the gratification of the physical sensations of the body, but by the subtle etheric exchange of magnetism and intellectual and spiritual polarization. This lifted the cult of Aphrodite out of the sphere of simple sensuality and explains why the priestesses of the cult commanded respect and were by no means looked upon as common prostitutes, although they received all who sought them. They were engaged in ministering to certain of the subtler needs of the human soul by means of their skilled arts. We have brought to a higher pitch of development than was ever known to the Greeks the art of stimulating desire with film and revue and syncopation, but we have no knowledge of the far more important art of meeting the needs of the human soul for etheric and mental interchange of magnetism, and it is for this reason that our sex life, both physiologically and socially, is so unstable and unsatisfactory.

We cannot understand sex aright unless we realize that it is one aspect of what the esotericist calls polarity, and that this is a principle that runs through the whole of creation, and is, in fact, the basis of manifestation. It is represented on the Tree by the two Pillars of Severity and Mercy. The whole of the activity of force is comprised in the principle of polarity, just as the whole of the function of form is comprised in the principle of metabolism.

Polarity really means the flowing of force from a sphere of high pressure to a sphere of low pressure; high and low being always relative terms. Every sphere of energy needs to receive the stimulus of an influx of energy at higher pressure, and to have an output into a sphere of lower pressure. The source of all energy is in the Great Unmanifest, and it makes its way down the levels, changing its form from one to the other, until it is finally "earthed" in Malkuth. In every individual life, in every form of activity, in every organized social group for whatever purpose, whether army, church, or limited company, we see the exemplification of this flowing of energy in circuit. The great point we need to realize is that in the microcosmic Tree there is a flow down and up the positive and negative aspects of our own subjective levels of consciousness, whereby the spirit inspires mind, and mind directs the emotions, and the emotions form the etheric double, and the etheric double molds the physical vehicle, which is the "earth" of the circuit. This is a fact that is generally realized, and its implications are easily seen as soon as attention is drawn to them.

But a point we do not so readily realize is that there is a flow and return between each "body" or level of consciousness and its corresponding aspect in the macrocosm. Just as there is an intake and output on the level of Malkuth whereby food and water are received into the body as nutriment and rejected as excreta, which is the food of the vegetable kingdom under the polite name of manure-so is there an intake and output between the etheric double and the astral light, and between the astral body and the mind side of nature, and so on up the planes, with the subtler factors represented by the Six higher Sephiroth.

The essence of the Magical Qabalah, which is the practical application of the Tree of Life, is to develop these magnetic circuits of the different levels, and so strengthen and reinforce the soul. Just as the physical body is nourished by eating and drinking, and kept healthy by adequate excretion, which might be called the operations of the Sphere of Malkuth, so is the soul of man energized by the operations of the Sphere of Tiphareth, which is also called the Sphere of the Redeemer, who brings health to the soul. We know how initiation develops the powers of the higher psychism and enables the human understanding to apprehend spiritual truths; what we do not realize is that for the full gamut of human development we need also to develop our power to contact natural energy in its essential form as represented by the Sphere of Netzach. We are accustomed to take the line that the spiritual and the natural are mutually antagonistic and that we must rob Peter to pay Paul, and to conclude that if the spiritual is the highest good, the natural must necessarily be the lowest evil; we do not realize that matter is crystallized spirit, and spirit is volatilized matter, and that there is no difference of substance between them, any more than there is between water and ice, but both are different states of the One Thing, as the alchemists call it; this is the great secret of alchemy which forms the philosophic basis of the secret doctrine of transmutation.

But the transmutation of metals is of little save academic importance compared to the transmutation of energy within the soul. It is this that the initiates deal with by means of the technique of the Tree of Life; and as consciousness transmutes up and down the Central Pillar of Mildness, or Equilibrium, so does energy transmute up and down the Pillar of Mercy, of which Netzach is the base, and form transmute up and down the Pillar of Severity, of which Hod, the intellect, is the base.

In Chokmah, then, we get the tremendous drive of life, which is the great male potency of the universe; in Chesed we get the organization of forces into interacting wholes; and in Netzach we get a sphere wherein evolution, ascending from Malkuth as organized force ensouling vivified form, is

able to contact essential force once more.
Netzach, the Sphere of Nogah, which is the
Hebrew name for Venus-Aphrodite, is
therefore an exceedingly important Sphere
from the point of view of the practical work
of occultism. It is because most people who
go in for occultism work up the Central Pillar
only, which is the Pillar of Consciousness, and
pay no attention to the side pillars, which are
the Pillars of Function, that such negligible
results are obtained from initiation. The blind
are leading the blind, and the average would-
be initiator in modern occult fraternities, who
is usually more of a mystic than an occultist,
does not realize that he has got to initiate
subconsciousness as well as consciousness,
and illuminate the instincts as well as the
reason.

We have considered Netzach from the
objective and the subjective points of view; it
now remains to study the symbolism assigned
to this Sephirah in the light of the knowledge
we have already obtained.

We shall observe at once that the symbolism
contains two distinct ideas-the idea of power
and the idea of beauty; and we are reminded
of the love that existed between Venus and
Mars according to the old myth. Now these
myths are not fabulous, save in the historical
sense, but represent truths of the spirit; and

when we find the same idea recurring in different pantheons, when we find Hebrew Qabalist and Greek poets, whose mentalities were as far removed from each other as the poles, presenting the same concept in different forms, we must conclude that it is not accidental, but will repay careful scrutiny.

Let us depart from our usual method of analyzing the symbols in the given order and classify them according to the two types into which they fall.

The Hebrew title of the Seventh Sephirah is Netzach, meaning Victory. Its additional title is Firmness, which carries out the same idea of masterful and victorious energy.
The God-name is Jehovah Tzabaoth, meaning the Lord of Hosts, or God of Armies. The Order of Angels assigned to Netzach are the Elohim, or gods, the rulers of Nature. The four Tarot cards assigned to this Sephirah all contain the idea of battle, even if in a negative form. It is curious to note, however, that it is only the Seven of Wands which has a good, or positive, significance. The other three Sevens are all cards of ill fortune. The reason for this becomes clear, however, when we understand the symbolism as a whole, so we will put it aside for the moment, and reconsider it later.

Let us now turn to the consideration of the other set of symbolic images. The Mundane Chakra of Netzach is the planet Venus, and the magical image is, appropriately enough, "a beautiful naked woman". The spiritual experience assigned to this sphere is the Vision of Beauty Triumphant. The virtue is Unselfishness-that is to say, the capacity to polarize from the negative pole. The vices are the obvious ones of love abused- unchastity and lust.

The correspondence in the microcosm is with the loins, hips, and legs. These, it will be noted, form the setting of the generative organs, but not the generative organs themselves, and bear out the idea previously shadowed forth, that the goddess of Love and the fertility goddess are not one and the same thing.

The symbols assigned to Netzach are the Lamp, the Girdle, and the Rose. The Girdle and Rose are self-explanatory, for they are traditionally associated with Venus. The Lamp, however, requires more explanation, for the classical associations afford us no clue on this point. We must turn to alchemy.

The four Elements are associated with the four lower Sephiroth, and of these the Element of Fire is associated with

Netzach. The Lamp is the magical weapon used in operations of the Element of Fire. Hence the association with Netzach.

The Element of Fire is associated with the fiery energy at the heart of Nature and connects up with the Mars aspect of the Venus Sephirah.

We see, then, from a study of the foregoing symbolism, that the Mars, or Victory, symbolism is associated with the Macrocosm, and the Venus, or Love symbolism, with the Microcosmic or subjective aspect. This gives us the key to a very important psychological truth, well understood by the ancients, but which had to await the work of Freud for its interpretation in modern language. This may best be expressed by saying that elemental energy, or the fundamental dynamism of an individual, is very closely connected with the sex life of that individual.

This is a very important fact in our psychic life, well understood by psychologists though but little appreciated by mystics and psychics, who generally incline to an idealism which seeks to escape from matter and its problems. But to escape like this is to leave unconquered fortresses in our rear; and the wiser way, the only way that can produce wholeness of life and a balanced temperament, is to give due

124

place to Netzach, which balances the intellectuality of Hod and the materiality of Malkuth, remembering always that the Tree consists of the two Pillars of Polarity and the Path of Equilibrium between them.

The true secret of natural goodness lies in the recognition of the contending rights of the Pairs of Opposites; there is no such antinomy as between Good and Evil, but only the balance between two extremes, each of which is evil when carried to excess, both of which give rise to evil if insufficient for equipoise. Unbridled license leads to degradation; but unbalanced idealism leads to psychopathology.

There are three types of persons who pass within the Veil - the mystic, the psychic, and the occultist. The mystic aspires to union with God and achieves his end by putting aside all that is not of God in his life. The psychic is a receiver of subtle vibrations, but not a transmitter. The occultist must need be to some extent at least, a receiver, but his primary aim is to be able to control and direct in the invisible kingdoms in the same way that the man of science has learnt to control and direct in the kingdom of Nature.

In order to achieve this end, he must work in harmony with the invisible forces in the same way that the scientist masters Nature by understanding her. Of these invisible forces, some are spiritual, descending from Kether, and some are elemental, working up from Malkuth. The Kether forces of the Macrocosm are picked up by the Tiphareth-center in the Microcosm, to use the Qabalistic terminology; the elemental forces are picked up by the Yesod-center, but-and this is the important point-they are directed and controlled by the manner in which the equilibrium is maintained between Netzach and Hod.

Netzach, in the Microcosm, represents the instinctive, emotional side of our nature, and Hod represents the intellect; Netzach is the artist in us, and Hod is the scientist. According as our moods shift between restraint and dynamism will he the polarity of Hod and Netzach in the Microcosm, which is the soul. If there is no Netzach influence to introduce a dynamic element, the over-preponderance of Hod will lead to all theory and no practice in occult matters. No one can handle magic in whom the Sphere of Netzach is not in function, for the skepticism of Hod will kill all magical images before their birth. Like all things in nature, Hod, unfertilized by its opposing polarity, is sterile. There must be something of the artist in every occultist who wants to do practical work. The intellect alone, however powerful, does not confer powers. It is through the Netzach in our own nature that the elemental forces obtain access to consciousness; without Netzach, they remain in the subconscious Sphere of Yesod, working blindly. It is taught in the Mysteries that each level of manifestation has its own ethic, or standard of right and wrong, and that we must not confuse the planes by expecting from one the standard of another, which is not applicable thereon. In the realm of mind, the ethic is Truth; on the astral plane, which is the sphere of the emotions and instincts, the ethic is Beauty. We must learn to understand the righteousness of Beauty, as well as the beauty of righteousness, if we want to bring all the provinces of the inner kingdom into obedience to the central power of unified consciousness.

In entering upon the region of the four lower Sephiroth we are coming into the sphere of the human mind. Subjectively considered, they constitute the personality and its powers. It is the aim of occult initiation to develop these powers and, if taken from the higher standpoint, as it always should be if it is not to degenerate into black magic, to unite them with Tiphareth, which is the focusing-point of the higher self, or Individuality. In discussing Netzach, therefore, we have definitely passed within the portal of the Mysteries, and are treading upon the sacred ground reserved for initiates.

I am no advocate of a secrecy which is simply priestcraft, but there are certain practical secrets of the Mysteries which it is inadvisable to cry aloud lest they be abused. There is also the inveterate tendency of human nature to apply its own definitions to familiar terms, and to refuse to recognize them apart from their familiar associations. If I lift a corner of the Veil of the Temple and reveal the fact that sex is simply a special instance of the universal principle of polarity, the immediate assumption is that polarity and sex are synonymous terms. If I say that although sex is a part of polarity, there is a great deal of polarity that has nothing to do with sex, my explanation is ignored. Perhaps I shall be understood better if I substitute the terminology of physics for that of the more appropriate psychology and say that life will only flow in circuit; insulate it, and it becomes inert. Let us take the human personality as an electrical machine; it must be connected up with the power-house, which is God, the Source of all Life, or there will be no motive power; but equally it must be "earthed," or the power will not flow. Every human being must be "earthed" to the earth, both literally and metaphorically. The idealist tries to induce a complete insulation of all earth-contacts in order that the inflowing power may not be wasted; he fails to realize that the earth is one great magnet.

Tradition declares from of old that the key to the Mysteries was written upon the Emerald Tablet of Hermes, whereon were inscribed the words, "As above, so below." Apply the principles of physics to psychology, and the riddle will be read. He that hath ears to hear, let him hear.

Finally, we come to the consideration of the significance of the Tarot cards associated with Netzach. These are the four Sevens of the Tarot pack.

As we are now coming within the sphere of influence of the earth-plane, it may be as well to explain what these lesser cards of the Tarot pack represent in divination. They symbolize the different modes of function of the different Sephirothic forces in the four worlds of the Qabalists. The suit of Wands corresponds to the spiritual level; Cups to the mental level; Swords to the astral plane; and Pentacles to the physical plane. Consequently, if the Seven of Pentacles turns up in a divination, it means that the influence of Netzach is playing a part on the physical level. There is an old proverb, "Lucky in love, unlucky at cards," which is but another way of saying that the person who is attractive to the opposite sex is usually in perpetual hot water. Venus is a disturbing influence in worldly affairs. She distracts from the serious business of life. As soon as her influence comes through to Malkuth, she must hand over the scepter to Ceres and leave well alone. It is children, not love, that keep the home together. The Qabalistic name of the Seven of Pentacles is "Success Unfulfilled," and we have only to look at the lives of Cleopatra, Guinevere, Iseult, Heloise to realize that Venus upon the physical plane has for her motto, "All for love, and the world well lost."

The suit of Swords is assigned to the astral plane. The secret title of the Seven of Swords is "Unstable Effort." How well does this express the action of Venus in the sphere of the emotions, with its short-lived intensity.

The secret title of the Seven of Cups is "Illusory Success." This card represents the working of Venus in the sphere of mind, where her influence is by no means conducive to clear-sightedness. We believe what we want to believe when we are under the influence of Venus. Upon this plane her motto might well be "Love is blind."

Only in the sphere of the spirit does Venus come into her own. Here her card, the Seven of Wands, is called "Valor," which well describes the dynamic and vitalizing influence she exerts when her spiritual significance is understood and employed.

Very interestingly do the four Tarot cards assigned to Netzach reveal the nature of the Venusian influence as it comes, down the planes. They teach us a very important lesson, for they show how essentially unstable this force is unless it is rooted in spiritual principle. The lower forms of love are of the emotions, and essentially unreliable; but the higher love is dynamic and energizing.

The Sixth Dimension

Tiphareth

There are three important keys to the nature of Tiphareth. Firstly, it is the center of equilibrium of the whole tree, being in the middle of the Central Pillar; secondly, it is Kether on a lower arc and Yesod on a higher arc; thirdly, it is the point of transmutation between the planes of force and the planes of form. The titles that are bestowed on it in Qabalistic nomenclature bear this out. From the point of view of Kether, it is a child; from the point of view of Malkuth, it is a king; and from the point of view of the transmutation of force it is a sacrificed god.

Macrocosmically, that is to say, from the Kether standpoint, Tiphareth is the equilibrium of Chesed and Geburah; microcosmically, that is to say from the point of view of transcendental psychology, it is the point where the types of consciousness characteristic of Kether and Yesod are brought to a focus. Hod and Netzach equally find their synthesis in Tiphareth.

The six Sephiroth, of which Tiphareth is the center, are sometimes called Adam Kadmon, the archetypal man; in fact, Tiphareth cannot rightly be understood, save as the central point of these six, wherein it rules as a king in his kingdom. It is these six which, for all practical purposes, constitute the archetypal kingdom which lies behind the kingdom of form in Malkuth and completely dominates and determines the passivities of matter.

When we have to consider a Sephirah in relation to its neighbors in order to interpret in the light of its position on the Tree, it is not possible to proceed with an entirely systematic and orderly exposition of the Qabalistic system, for we must of necessity, forestall with partial explanations, if our argument is to be comprehensible. We must therefore give some explanation of the three lower Sephiroth grouped around Tiphareth, Netzach, Hod, and Yesod.

Netzach is concerned with the Nature forces and elemental contacts; Hod with ceremonial magic and occult knowledge; and Yesod with psychism and the etheric double. Tiphareth itself, supported by Geburah and Gedulah, represents seership, or the higher psychism of the individuality. Each Sephirah, of course, has its subjective and objective aspects-its factor in psychology and its plane in the universe.

The four Sephiroth below Tiphareth represent the personality, or lower self; the four Sephiroth above Tiphareth are the Individuality, or higher self, and Kether is the Divine Spark, or nucleus of manifestation.

Tiphareth, therefore, must never be regarded as an isolated factor, but as a link, a focusing-point, a center of transition or transmutation. The Central Pillar is always concerned with consciousness. The two side Pillars with the different modes of the operation of force on the different levels.

In Tiphareth we find the archetypal ideals brought to a focus and transmuted into archetypal ideas. It is, in fact, the Place of Incarnation. For this reason, it is called the Child. And because incarnation of the god-ideal also implies the sacrificial disincarnation, to Tiphareth are assigned the Mysteries of the

Crucifixion, and all the Sacrificed Gods are placed here when the Tree is applied to the pantheons. God the Father is assigned to Kether; but God the Son is assigned to Tiphareth, for the reasons given above.

Exoteric religion goes no further up the Tree than Tiphareth. It has no understanding of the mysteries of creation as represented by the symbolism of Kether, Chokmah, and Binah; nor of the modes of operation of the Dark and Bright Archangels as represented in the symbolism of Geburah and Gedulah; nor of the mysteries of consciousness and the transmutation of force as represented in the invisible Sephirah Daath, which has no symbolism.

In Tiphareth, God is made manifest in form and dwells among us; i.e. comes within range of human consciousness. Tiphareth, the Son, "shows us" Kether, the Father. So, then, we understand: **"Jesus saith unto him, I am the way, the truth, and the life: no man cometh unto the Father, but by me"** – to read, Jesus (the Son, or Tiphareth) says there is no way to the Father, or Kether, than through me.

In order that form may be stabilized, the component forces out of which it is built must be brought into equilibrium. Therefore, do we find the idea of the Mediator, or Redeemer, inherent in this Sephirah. When the Godhead in its very Self manifests in form, that form must be perfectly equilibrated. One might with equal truth, reverse the proposition and say that when the forces building a form are perfectly equilibrated, the Godhead, its very Self, is manifesting in that form according to its type. God is made manifest among us when the conditions permit of manifestation.

Having come through into manifestation on the planes of form in the Child aspect of Tiphareth, the incarnated god grows to manhood and becomes the Redeemer. In other words, having obtained incarnation by means of matter in a virgin state, i.e. Mary, Marah, the Sea, the Great Mother, Binah, a Supernal, as distinguished from the Inferior Mother, Malkuth, the developing God-manifestation, is forever striving to bring the Kingdom of the six central Sephiroth into a state of equilibrium.

When the glyph of the Fall is represented upon the Tree, it is interesting to note that the heads of the Great Serpent that rise out of Chaos, only come as far as Tiphareth, and do not overpass it.

The Redeemer, then, manifests in Tiphareth, and is forever striving to redeem His Kingdom by re-uniting it to the Supernals across the gulf made by the Fall, which separated the lower Sephiroth from the higher, and by bringing the diverse forces of the sixfold kingdom into equilibrium.

To this end are the incarnated gods sacrificed, dying for the people, in order that the tremendous emotional force set free by this act may compensate the unbalanced force of the Kingdom, and thus, redeem it or bring it into equilibrium.

It is this Sphere on the Tree that is called the Christ-center, and it is here that the Christian religion has its focusing-point. The pantheistic faiths, such as the Greek and Egyptian, center in Yesod; and the metaphysical faiths, such as the Buddhist and Confucian, aim at Kether. But as all religions worthy of the name, have both an esoteric, or mystical, and an exoteric, or pantheistic, aspect. Christianity, although it is essentially a Tiphareth faith, has its mystical aspect centering in Kether, and its magical aspect, as seen in popular continental Catholicism, centering in Yesod. Its evangelical aspect aims at a concentration on Tiphareth as Child and Sacrificed God and ignores the aspect of the King in the center of his Kingdom, surrounded by the five Holy Sephiroth of manifestation.

Hitherto, we have considered the Tree from the macrocosmic point of view, seeing the different archetypes of manifesting force come into action and build the universe, and have but remotely approached them from the microcosmic point of view, in their psychological aspect as factors in consciousness. But with Tiphareth, our mode of approach changes, for from henceforward, the archetypal forces are locked up in forms, and can only be approached from the point of view of their effect upon consciousness; in other words, our mode of approach must now be through the direct experience of the senses, though these senses are not of the physical plane only, but function in both Tiphareth and Yesod, each according to type. While we were on the higher levels we had to rely on metaphysical analogy and reasoning by deduction from first principles; now we are within the legitimate field of inductive science, and must submit ourselves to its discipline and express our findings in its terms; but at the same time we must maintain our link with the transcendentals through Tiphareth; this is achieved by expressing the symbolism of Tiphareth in terms of mystical experience. All mystical experiences of the type in which the vision ends in blinding light are assigned to

Tiphareth; for the fading-out of form in the overwhelming influx of force, characterizes the transitional mode of consciousness of this Sphere on the Tree. Visions which maintain clearly outlined form throughout are characteristic of Yesod. Illuminations which have no form, such as those described by Plotinus, are rising towards Kether.

In Tiphareth, also are gathered up and interpreted the operations of the nature magic of Netzach, and the Hermetic magic of Hod. Both these operations are in terms of form, though form predominates in the operation of Hod, to a greater degree than in those of Netzach. All the astral visions of Yesod also must be translated into terms of metaphysics, via the mystical experiences of Tiphareth. If this translation is not made, we become hallucinated; for we think the reflections cast into the mirror of the subconscious mind and translated there into terms of brain-consciousness are the actual things of which they are really only the symbolic representations.

Kether is metaphysical; Yesod is psychic; and Tiphareth is essentially mystical; mystical being understood as a mode of mentation in which consciousness ceases to work in symbolic subconscious representations but apprehends by means of emotional reactions.

The different additional titles and symbolism assigned to the various Sephiroth, and especially the God-names thereof, give us a very important key for the unlocking of the mysteries of the Bible, which is essentially a Qabalistic book. According to the manner in which Deity is referred to, we know to what Sphere on the Tree the particular mode of manifestation should be assigned. All references to the Son always refer to Tiphareth; all references to the Father refer to Kether; all references to the Holy Ghost refer to Yesod; and very deep mysteries are concealed here, for the Holy Ghost is the aspect of the Godhead that is worshipped in the occult lodges; the worship of pantheistic nature-forces and elemental operations take place under the presidency of God the Father; and the regenerative ethical aspect of religion, which is the exoteric aspect for this epoch, is under the presidency of God the Son in Tiphareth.

The initiate, however, transcends his epoch, and aims at uniting all three modes of adoration in his worship of Deity, as a trinity in unity; the Son redeeming the pantheistic nature worship from debasement, and making the transcendental Father comprehensible to human consciousness, for "whoso hath seen Me, hath seen the Father."

Tiphareth, however, is not only the center of the Sacrificed God, but also the center of the Inebriating God, the Giver of Illumination.

Dionysus is assigned to this center as well as Osiris, for, as we have already seen, the Central Pillar is concerned with the modes of consciousness; and human consciousness, rising from Yesod by the Path of the Arrow, receives illumination in Tiphareth; therefore, all the givers of illumination in the Pantheons are assigned to Tiphareth.

Illumination consists of the introduction of the mind to a higher mode of consciousness than that which is built up out of sensory experience. In illumination, the mind changes gear, as it were. Unless, however, the new mode of consciousness is connected up with the old and translated into terms of finite thought, it remains as a flash of light so brilliant that it blinds. We do not see by means of the ray of light that shines upon us, but by means of the amount of that ray which is reflected from objects of our own dimension upon which it lights. Unless there are ideas in our minds which are illuminated by this higher mode of consciousness, our minds are merely overwhelmed, and the darkness is more intense to our eyes after that blinding experience of a high mode of consciousness than it was before. In fact, we do not so much change gear as throw the engine of our mind out of gear altogether. This, for the most part, is what so-called illumination amounts to. There is enough of a flash to convince us of the reality of super-physical existence, but not enough to teach us anything of its nature.

The importance of the Tiphareth stage in mystical experience lies in the fact that the incarnation of the Child takes place here; in other words, mystical experience gradually builds up a body of images and ideas that are lit up and made visible when illuminations take place.

This Child aspect of Tiphareth is also a very important one to us in such practical work of the Mysteries as is concerned with illumination. For we must accept the fact that the Child-Christ does not spring like Minerva, full-armed from the head of God the Father, but starts as a small thing, humbly laid among the beasts, and not even housed in the with the humans. The first glimpses of mystical experience must perforce be very limited because we have not had time to build up through experience a body of images and ideas that shall serve to represent them. These can only be got together with time, each transcendental experience adding its quota and subsequent rational meditation organizing them.

Mystics are very apt to make the mistake of thinking that they are following the Star to the place of the Sermon on the Mount, not to the Manger at Bethlehem, the birthplace. It is here that the method of the Tree is so valuable, enabling the transcendent to be expressed in terms of symbolism, and symbolism to be translated into terms of metaphysics; thus, linking the psychic with the spiritual via the intellect, and bringing all three aspects of our trinitarian consciousness into focus.

It is in Tiphareth that this translation is made, for in Tiphareth are received the mystical experiences of direct consciousness which illuminate the psychic symbols.

The Central Pillar of the Tree is essentially the Pillar of Consciousness, just as the two side Pillars are the Pillars of the active and passive powers. When considered microcosmically, that is to say from the point of view of psychology, instead of cosmology, Kether, the Divine Spark round which the individualized being builds up, must be regarded as the nucleus of consciousness rather than consciousness itself. Daath, the invisible Sephirah, is also on the Central Pillar, though, strictly speaking, it always belongs to another plane to that on which the Tree is being considered. For instance, as we are considering the Tree microcosmically at the moment, Daath would be the point of contact with the macrocosm. It is not until we come to Tiphareth that we get clear-cut, individualized consciousness.

Tiphareth is the functional apex of the Second Triad on the Tree, whose two basal angles consist of Geburah and Gedulah (Chesed). This Second Triad, emanating from the First Triad of the Three Supernals, forms the evolving individuality, or spiritual soul. It is this which endures and builds up throughout an evolution; it is from this that the successive personalities, the units of incarnation, are emanated; it is into this that the active essence of experience is absorbed at the end of each incarnation when the incarnating unit dissolves into dust and ether.

It is this Second Triad which forms the Oversoul, the Higher Self, the Holy Guardian Angel, the First Initiator. It is the voice of this higher self, which is so often heard with the inner ear, and not the voice of discarnate entities, or of God Himself, as is thought by those who have had no training in tradition.

Overshadowed and directed by the Second Triad, the Third Triad builds up through the experience of incarnation, with Malkuth as its physical vehicle. Brain consciousness is of Malkuth, and as long as we are imprisoned in Malkuth, that is all we have. But the doors of Malkuth are not closely shut nowadays, and many there are who can peer through the crack at the phantasmagoria of the astral plane and experience the psychic consciousness of Yesod. When this has been achieved, the way opens for the higher psychism, the true seership, which is characteristic of the consciousness of Tiphareth.

Our first experience of the higher psychism, therefore, is usually in terms of the lower psychism to commence with; for we have only just risen clear of Malkuth and are looking up at the Sun of Tiphareth from the Moon-sphere of Yesod. Therefore, we hear voices with the inner ear and see visions with the inner eye, but they differ from ordinary psychic consciousness because they are not the direct representations of astral forms, but symbolic presentations of spiritual things, in terms of astral consciousness. This is a normal function of the subconscious mind, and it is very important that it should be thoroughly understood, for misconceptions on this point give rise to very serious problems and may even lead to mental unbalance.

Those who are familiar with Qabalistic terminology know that the first of the greater

initiations is said to consist of the power to
enjoy the knowledge and conversation of our
Holy Guardian Angel; this Holy Guardian
Angel, be it remembered, is really our own
higher self. It is the prime characteristic of
this higher mode of mentation that it consists
neither in voices nor visions but is pure
consciousness; it is an intensification of
awareness, and from this quickening of the
mind comes a peculiar power of insight and
penetration which is of the nature of hyper-
developed intuition. The higher consciousness
is never psychic, but always intuitive,
containing no sensory imagery. It is this
absence of sensory imagery which tells the
experienced initiate that he is on the level of
the higher consciousness.

The ancients recognized this, and they
differentiated between the mantic methods
which induced the chthonic, or underworld
contacts, and the divine inebriation of the
Mysteries. The Monads, rushing in the train of
Dionysus, were of an entirely different order
of initiation to the pythonesses; the
pythonesses were psychics and mediums, but
the Monads, the initiates of the Dionysiac
Mysteries, enjoyed exaltation of consciousness
and a quickening of life that enabled them to
perform amazing prodigies of strength.
All the dynamic religions have this Dionysiac
aspect; even in the Christian religion many

saints have left record of the Crucified Christ of their devotion coming to them at last as the Divine Bridegroom; and when they speak of this divine inebriation that comes to them, their language uses the metaphors of human love as its appropriate expression- "How lovely art thou, my sister, my spouse."- "Faint from the kisses of the lips of God . . ." These things tell a great deal to those who have understanding.

The Dionysiac aspect of religion represents an essential factor in human psychology, and it is the misunderstanding of this factor, which upon the one hand, prevents the manifestation of the higher spiritual experiences in our modern civilization, and upon the other, permits of the strange aberrations of religious feeling that from time to time give rise to scandal and tragedy in the high places of the more dynamic religious movements.

There is a certain emotional concentration and exaltation which makes the higher phases of consciousness available, and without which it is impossible to attain them. The images of the astral plane pass over into an intensity of emotion that is like a burning fire, and when all the dross of the nature has gone up in flame the smoke clears, and we are left with the white heat of pure consciousness. By the very nature of the human mind, with the brain as its instrument, this white heat cannot endure for long; but in the brief space of its lasting, changes occur in the temperament, and the mind itself receives new concepts and undergoes an expansion that never wholly retracts. The tremendous exaltation of the experience dies away, but we are left with a permanent expansion of personality, an enhanced capacity for life in general, and a power of realization of spiritual realities which could never have been ours if we had not been swung forcibly across the great gulf of consciousness by the momentum of ecstasy.

Modern spiritual leaders have no knowledge of the technique of the deliberate production of ecstasy and no idea how to direct it when it occurs spontaneously. Revivalists succeed in producing a mild form of it among unsophisticated people, by means of personal magnetism, and the worth of a revivalist is judged by his power to inebriate his hearers. But the consequences of this inebriation are apt to be like the consequences of any other inebriation, and life seems exceedingly stale, flat, and unprofitable when the revivalist moves on to other fields of activity. Because the inebriation dies away, the convert thinks he has lost God; no one seems to realize that ecstasy is a magnesium flash in consciousness, and if it were prolonged, would burn up the brain and nervous system. But although it cannot be, and is not meant to be, prolonged, by means of it we swing over the dead center of consciousness and awake to a higher life.

The technique of the Tree gives accurate definition to these spiritual experiences, and those who are trained in that technique do not mistake the stirring of their own higher consciousness for the voice of God. From the sensory consciousness of Malkuth, through the astral psychism of Yesod, to the formless intuitions and quickened consciousness of Tiphareth, they rise and descend smoothly and skillfully; never confusing the planes or suffering them to leak one into another, but bringing them all into focus in a centralized consciousness.

Tiphareth is called by the Qabalists, Shemesh, or the Sphere of the Sun; and it is interesting to note that all sun-gods are healing gods, and all healing gods are sun-gods, a fact which affords us food for thought.

The sun is the central point of our existence. Without the sun there would be no solar system. Sunlight plays a very important part in the metabolism, the life-process, of living creatures, and the whole of the nutrition of green plants depends upon it. Its influence is closely allied to that of vitamins, as is proved by the fact that certain vitamins can be used to supplement its activities. We see, therefore, that sunlight is a very important factor in our well-being; we might go even further and say that it is essential to our very existence and that our association with the sun is far more intimate than we realize.

The symbol of the sun in the mineral kingdom is gold, pure and precious, which all nations have agreed in calling the metal of the sun, and recognizing as the most precious metal and the basic unit of exchange. The part played by gold in the polity of nations far exceeds its intrinsic utility as a metal. It is, moreover, the one substance on earth which is incorruptible, and impossible to be tarnished. It may be dulled by the accumulation of dirt upon its surface, but the metal itself, unlike silver or iron, undergoes no chemical change or decomposition. Neither does water corrode it.

The sun is to us truly the Giver of Life and source of all being; it is the only adequate symbol of God the Father, who may aptly be called the Sun behind the Sun, Tiphareth, in fact, being the immediate reflection of Kether. It is through the mediation of the sun that life comes to the earth, and it is by means of the Tiphareth consciousness that we contact the sources of vitality and draw upon them, both consciously and unconsciously.

The sun is, above all things, the symbol of manifesting energy; it is sudden, unaccustomed gushes of solar-spiritual energy that cause the divine inebriation of ecstasy; it is gold, as the basis of money, which is the objective representative of externalized life-force; for verily, money is life and life is money, for without money we can have no fullness of life. Life-force, manifesting on the physical plane as energy and on the mental plane as intelligence and knowledge, can be transmuted by the appropriate alchemy into money, which is a token of the capacity or energy of someone. Money is the symbol of human energy, by means of which we can store up our output of work hour by hour, receiving it back as wages at the end of the week, and spending it on necessities or saving it for future use, as we think fit. The gold which backs the notes is a symbol of human energy, and is only earned by an expenditure of that energy; though it may be the energy of a father or a husband, transmitted through an heiress, yet nevertheless it is the symbol of some human being's activity in some sphere, even if it be only the sphere of company-promoting or burglary.

The secret, underground movements of gold act in the polity of nations, as hormones act in the human body, and there are cosmic laws governing their tidal and epochal movements which economists do not suspect.

Kether, Space, the source of all existence, reflects into Tiphareth, which acts as a transformer and distributor of the primal, spiritual energy. We receive this energy directly by means of sunlight, and indirectly by means of the chlorophyll in green plants, which enables them to utilize sunlight, and which we eat at first hand in vegetable foods, and at second hand in the tissues of herbivorous creatures.

But the Sun-god is more than the source of life. He is also the healer, when life goes wrong. For it is life, plus, minus, or misdirected, which is the activity in disease processes; disease has no energy, save what it borrows from the life of the organism. It is therefore by adjustments in the life-force that healing must be brought about, and the sun-gods are the natural gods to invoke in this connection, for life and the sun are so intimately connected.

It is by means of their knowledge of the manipulation of the solar influence that the ancient initiate-priests performed their

healings, and sun-worship lay at the root of
the Aesculapian cult of ancient Greece.

We moderns have learnt the value of sunlight
and vitamins in our physiological economy,
but we have not realized the very important
part played by the spiritual aspect of the solar
influences in our psychic economy, using that
word in its dictionary sense. There is a
Tiphareth factor in the soul of man which,
according to ancient tradition, has its physical
correspondence in the solar plexus, not in the
head or the heart, which is able to pick up the
subtle aspect of the solar energy in the same
way that the chlorophyll in the leaf of a plant
picks up its more tangible aspect. If we are cut
off from this energy and prevented from
assimilating it, we become as sickly and feeble
in mind and body as plants growing in a cellar,
cut off from its more tangible aspect.

This cutting-off from the spiritual aspect of
Nature is due to mental attitudes. When we
refuse to acknowledge our part in Nature, and
Nature's part in us, we inhibit this free flow of
life-giving magnetism between the part and
the whole; and lacking certain elements
essential to spiritual function, psychic health is
impossible.

Psycho-analysts attach great importance to
repression as a cause of psychic disease; they

learnt to recognize repression because in the extreme form of sex-repression its ill effects are conspicuous. They did not realize, however, that sex-repression, unless it is caused by circumstances, in which case it does not give rise to dissociation, is but the result of a cause which lies far deeper than sex, and has its roots in a false spirituality, a spurious refinement and idealism, which has led to the cutting-off of the sympathies, of the recognition, of the gratitude of a living creature from the Giver of Life, the higher aspect of Nature. This is caused by a spiritual vanity which considers the more primitive aspects of nature as beneath its dignity.

It is because of our spurious ideals with their false values that we have so much neurotic ill-health in our midst. It is because Priapus and Cloacina are not given their due as deities that we are cursed by the Sun-god and cut off from Its benign influence, for an insult to His subsidiary aspects, is an insult to Him.

When a creature is not in a fit state for reproduction, sexual advances are repellent to it; this is the natural basis of modesty and protects the organism from waste and exhaustion. Because an accumulation of decomposing excreta gives rise to disease, the odor of their excreta is repulsive to living creatures of even the lowliest development, so that they avoid its neighborhood. Out of these two repulsions, so rational and valuable under natural conditions, under our artificial conditions of civilized life, all manner of irrational taboos have grown up. The repulsion is overdone, and no longer serves its biological purpose.

Our attitude towards two important sections of natural life implies that they are unnatural, debased, poisonous. Consequently, we cut ourselves off from the earth- contacts; then the circuit is broken, and the heavenly contacts also fail us. The cosmic current comes down from Kether, through Tiphareth and Yesod, into Malkuth; if the circuit be broken anywhere, it cannot function. True, it is impossible to totally break the circuit during life, for the life-processes are so deeply rooted in nature that we cannot altogether suppress them; but a mental attitude can cause such a kinking of the tube, as it were, can so insulate and inhibit, that only a scanty flow can be sucked through against resistance by the desperate organism.

In Tiphareth, the Sun Centre, we have the spiritual manifesting in the natural, and we should give reverence to the Sun-god as representing the naturalization of spiritual processes; the spiritualization of natural processes has had a good deal to answer for in the history of human suffering.

The symbols assigned to the Sixth Sephirah become a very illuminating study when we examine them in the light of what we now know about the significance of Tiphareth, for we have here a very clear example of the way in which the symbols assigned to a given Sephirah lace in and out, in and out, in long chains of interrelated associations.

The meaning of the Hebrew word Tiphareth is Beauty; and of the many definitions of beauty that have been proposed, the most satisfying is that which finds beauty to lie in a due and just proportion, whatever the beautiful thing may be, whether moral or material. It is interesting, therefore, to find the Sephirah of Beauty as the central point of equilibrium of the whole Tree, and that one of the two Spiritual Experiences assigned to Tiphareth is the Vision of the Harmony of Things.

It is curious that two separate and, at first sight, unrelated Spiritual Experiences should be assigned to Tiphareth; it is, in fact, the only Sphere on the Tree where this occurs. It is also unique in having several Magical Images assigned to it. We must therefore ask ourselves why it is that the central Sephirah has these multiple aspects. The answer is to be found in the Yetziratic Text assigned to Tiphareth, which declares that "The Sixth Path is called the Mediating Intelligence. A mediator is essentially a connecting link, an intermediary; consequently Tiphareth, in its central position, must be looked upon as a two-way switch, and we must consider it both as receiving the "influxes of the Emanations", and as "causing that influence to flow into all the reservoirs of the blessings." We may therefore look upon it as the outward manifestation of the five subtler Sephiroth, and also as the spiritual principle behind the four denser Sephiroth. If looked at from the side of form, it is force; if looked at from the side of force, it is form. It is, in fact, the archetypal Sephirah in which the great principles represented by the five higher Sephiroth are formulated into concepts; "In it are multiplied the influxes of the Emanations," as the Sepher Yetzirah declares.

The name Zoar Anpin, Lesser Countenance, as distinguished from Arik Anpin, the Vast Countenance, one of the titles of Kether, further bears out this idea. For the formless formulations of Kether take shape in this, the sphere of the higher mind. As previously noted, Kether is reflected into Tiphareth. The Ancient of Days sees Himself reflected as in a glass, and the reflected image of the Vast

Countenance is called the Lesser Countenance and the Son.

But although a lesser manifestation and a younger generation as viewed from above, Tiphareth is also Adam Kadmon, the Archetypal Man, when viewed from beneath-from the side, that is to say, of Yesod and Malkuth. Tiphareth is Malek, the King, the husband of Malkab, the Bride, which is one of the titles of Malkuth.

It is in Tiphareth that we find the archetypal ideas which form the invisible framework of the whole of manifested creation formulating and expressing the primary principles emanating from the subtler Sephiroth. It is, as it were, a Treasure-house of Images on a higher arc; but whereas the astral plane is peopled by images reflected from forms, the images of the Sphere of Tiphareth are those formulating, and as it were crystallizing out, from the spiritual emanations of the higher potencies.

Tiphareth mediates between the microcosm and the macrocosm; "As above, so below," is the keynote of the Sphere of Shemesh, wherein the Sun that is behind the sun focusses into manifestation.

In the anatomy of the Divine Man is the interpretation of all organization and evolution. In fact, the material universe is literally the organs and members of this Divine Man; and it is through an understanding of the soul of Adam Kadmon, which consists of the "influxes of the Emanations," that we can interpret His anatomy in terms of function, which is the only way in which anatomy can be intelligently appreciated. It is because science is content largely to be descriptive, and shrinks from purposive explanations, that it is so barren of all philosophical import.

In transcendental psychology, which is the anatomy of the microcosm, the breast is the correspondence assigned to Tiphareth. In the breast are the lungs and the heart, and immediately below these organs, and intimately connected with them and controlling them, is the greatest network of nerves in the body, known as the solar plexus, aptly so named by the ancient anatomists. The lungs maintain a singularly intimate relationship between the microcosm and the macrocosm by determining the ceaseless tidal motion of the atmosphere, in and out, in and out, that never ceases day or night, until the golden bowl is broken, and the silver cord is loosed, and we cease to breathe. The heart determines the circulation of the blood, and the blood, as Paracelsus[42] truly said, is a "singular fluid." Modern medicine knows well what sunlight means to the blood. It has also discovered that chlorophyll, which is the green substance in the leaves of plants which enables them to utilize the sunlight as their source of energy, has a very potent influence upon the blood-pressure.

The three Magical Images of Tiphareth are curious, for at first sight they are so utterly unrelated that each one appears to cancel out the others. But in the light of what we now know concerning Tiphareth, their significance and relationship appears clearly, speaking through the language of symbolism, especially when studied in the light of the life of Jesus Christ, the Son.

Tiphareth, being the first coagulation of the Supernals, is aptly represented as the new-born Child in the manger at Bethlehem; as the Sacrificed God he becomes the Mediator between God and man; and when He has risen from the dead He is as a king come to his kingdom. Tiphareth is the child of Kether and the king of Malkuth, and in His own sphere lie is sacrificed.

---

[42] Swiss physician, alchemist, theologian, and philosopher of the German Renaissance.

We shall not understand Tiphareth aright
unless we have some concept of the real
meaning of sacrifice, which is very different to
the popular one, which conceives of it as the
voluntary loss of something dear. Sacrifice is
the translation of force from one form to
another. There is no such thing as the total
destruction of force; however completely it
disappears from our ken, it maintains itself in
some other form according to the great
natural law of the conservation of energy,
which is the law that maintains our universe in
existence. Energy may be locked up in form,
and therefore static; or it may be free from its
bondage to form, and in circulation. When we
make a sacrifice of any sort, we take a static
form of energy, and by breaking up the form
that imprisons it, put it into free circulation in
the cosmos. That which we sacrifice in one
form, turns up again in due course in another
form. Apply this concept to the religious and
ethical ideas of sacrifice and some very
valuable clues are obtained.

The God-name of this sphere is Aloah Va
Daath, which associates it intimately with the
Invisible Sephirah that comes between it and
Kether. This Sephirah, as we have already
seen, may best be understood as
apprehension, the dawning of consciousness;
and we may interpret the phrase

"Tetragrammaton Aloah Va Daath" as "God made manifest in the sphere of mind."

In the microcosm, Tiphareth represents the higher psychism, the mode of consciousness of the individuality, the higher self. It is essentially the sphere of religious mysticism as distinguished from the magic and psychism of Yesod; for be it remembered, the Sephiroth of the Central Pillar of the Tree represent levels of consciousness, and the Sephiroth on the side pillars represent powers and modes of function. Tiphareth is also said to be the Sphere of the Greater Masters; it is the Temple not made with hands, eternal in the heavens and the Great White Lodge. It is here that the initiated adept functions when in the higher consciousness; here that he hopes to meet the Masters, and it is by means of the Name, and by an understanding of the significance of the Name of Aloah Va Daath that he opens up the higher consciousness.

For be it noted that it is only in proportion to the significance a word has for us that it becomes a Word of Power. The name of his victim is a word of power to a murderer; and such is its recognized potency that in some countries an instrument to register the changes of blood-pressure is attached to the arm of a suspect while he is being questioned by the police, and the name of the dead man, and other words connected with the crime, are suddenly whispered in his ear, and if these are "words of power" for him, the instrument registers it beyond all question.

It is popularly believed that Names of Power exercise direct influence over spirits, angels, demons and such-like, but this is not so. The Name of Power exercises its influence upon the magician, and by exalting and directing consciousness enables him to get into touch with the chosen type of spiritual influence; if he has had experience of that particular type of influence, the Word of Power will stir potent subconscious memories; if he has not, and approaches the matter in the unimaginative and incredulous spirit of the scholar, the "barbarous Names of Evocation" will be just hocus-pocus for him. But be it noted that to the believing Catholic, "hocus-pocus," which is the Protestant's name for deception and superstition, and from which is derived the word hoax, means "Hoc est Corpus," which is an altogether different story. So, much lies in the viewpoint in these matters.

Therefore, it is that a definite spiritual experience is assigned to each Sephirah, and until a person has had that experience he is not an initiate of that Sephirah, and cannot make use of its Names of Power even if he knows them. As tradition has it, it is not enough to know a Name of Power, one must also know how to vibrate it. It is generally believed that the vibration of a Name of Power is the right note on which to chant it; but magical vibration is something much more than that. When one is deeply moved, and at the same time devotionally exalted, the voice drops several tones below its normal pitch and becomes resonant and vibrant; it is this tremor of emotion combined with the resonance of devotion which constitutes the vibration of a Name, and this cannot be learnt or taught; it can only be spontaneous. It is like the wind, it bloweth where it listeth. When it comes, it shakes one from head to heel with a wave of fiery heat, and all who hear it involuntarily come to attention. It is an extraordinary experience to hear a Word of Power vibrated. It is an even more extraordinary experience to vibrate it.

The archangel of Tiphareth is Raphael, the "spirit that standeth in the sun," who is also the angel of healing.

When the initiate is "working on the Tree," that is to say is building up in his imagination a diagram of the Tree of Life in his aura, he formulates Tiphareth in his solar plexus between the abdomen and the breast; if he intends to work in the sphere of the Sixth

Sephirah, and concentrates the power in this center, he will find that he himself has suddenly become a spirit standing in the sun, with the blazing photosphere all around him. It is one thing to formulate a Sephirah in one's aura; but it is quite another to find oneself right inside the Sephirah. Although one can receive the influence of a Sephirah by means of the former operation, and it is a good routine method for daily meditation, it is not until one has everted-as it were, turned clean inside out, so that the position is reversed, and instead of the Sphere being inside one, one is inside the Sphere-that one can work with the power of a Sephirah. It is this experience which is the culmination of the initiation of a Sephirah.

The Order of Angels of Tiphareth are the Malachim, or Kings. These are the spiritual principles of natural forces--and no one can control, or even safely make contact with elemental principles unless he holds the initiation of Tiphareth, which is that of a minor adept. For he must have been accepted by the Elemental Kings, that is to say, he must have realized the ultimate spiritual nature of natural forces before he can handle them in their elemental form. In their subjective elemental form, they appear in the microcosm as powerful instincts of combat, of reproduction, of self-abasement, of self-

aggrandizement, and all those emotional
factors known to the psychologist. It is
obvious, therefore, that if we stir and
stimulate these emotions in our natures, it
must be in order that we may use them as
servants of the higher self, directed by reason
and spiritual principle. It is necessary,
therefore, that when we operate the elemental
forces, we do so through the Kings, under the
presidency of the Archangel and by the
invocation of the Holy Name of God
appropriate to the sphere. Microcosmically,
this means that the powerful elemental
driving-forces of our nature are correlated
with the higher self, instead of being
dissociated into the Qliphothic underworld of
the Freudian unconscious.

Elemental operations are not, of course,
performed in the Sphere of Tiphareth, but it
is essential that they should be controlled
from the Sphere of Tiphareth if they are to
remain White Magic. If there is no such
higher control, they will soon slide off into
Black Magic. It is said that at the Fall, the four
lower Sephiroth became detached from
Tiphareth and assimilated to the Qliphoth.

When the elemental forces become detached
from their spiritual principles in our concepts,
so that they become ends in themselves, even
if no evil, but merely experimentation is

intended, a Fall takes place and degeneration soon follows. But when we clearly realize the spiritual principle behind all natural things, they are then in a state of innocence, to use a theological term with a definite connotation; they are unfallen, and we can safely work with them and advantageously develop them in our own natures; thus, bringing about the unrepression and equilibrium so necessary to mental health. This correlation of the natural with the spiritual, thus maintaining it unfallen and in a state of innocence, is a very important point in all practical workings in any form of magic.

As has already been seen, two spiritual experiences go to make up the initiation of Tiphareth, the Vision of the Harmony of Things, and the Vision of the Mysteries of the Crucifixion, We have already seen in another connection that there are two aspects to Tiphareth, and therefore must be two Spiritual experiences in its initiation.

In the Vision of the Harmony of Things we see deep into the spiritual side of Nature; in other words, we meet the Angelic Kings, the Malachim. Through this experience we understand that the natural is but the dense aspect of the spiritual, the "Outer Robe of Concealment" covering the "Inner Robe of Glory." It is this understanding of the spiritual significance of the natural which is so lamentably lacking in our religious life today, and which is responsible for so much neurotic ill-health and so much married unhappiness.

It is through this Vision of the Harmony of Things that we are made one with Nature, not by means of elemental contacts. Human beings who are in anywise raised by culture above the primitive, cannot become one with Nature upon the elemental level, for to do so is degeneration, and they become beastly in both senses of the word. The nature contacts are made through the Angelic Kings of the Elements in the Sphere of Tiphareth-in other words, through the realization of the spiritual principles behind natural things-and the initiate then comes to the elemental beings in the name of their presiding King. He descends into the elemental kingdoms from above, as it were, bringing with him his manhood; thus, he is an initiator to the elementals; but if he meets them on their own level, he abrogates his manhood and returns to an earlier phase of evolution. Elemental force, not limited and kept in check by the limitations of an animal brain, is bound to be unbalanced force when it flows through the wide channels of a human intellect, and the result is chaos, which is one of the Kingdoms of the Qliphoth[43].

The Mysteries of the Crucifixion are both macrocosmic and microcosmic. In their macrocosmic aspect we find them in the myths of the Great Redeemers of mankind, who are always born of God and a Virgin mother, thus again emphasizing the dual nature of Tiphareth, wherein form and force meet together. But let us not forget their microcosmic aspect, as an experience of mystical consciousness. It is by means of an understanding of the Mysteries of the Crucifixion, which concern the magical power of sacrifice, that we are able to transcend the limitations of brain consciousness, limited to sensation and habituated to form, and enter into the wider consciousness of the higher psychism. We thus become able to transcend form and thereby release the latent force, changing it from static to kinetic, and rendering it available for the Great Work, which is regeneration.

The characteristic virtue of the Sphere of Tiphareth is Devotion to this Great Work. Devotion is a very important factor in the Way of Initiation that leads to the higher

---

[43] In Qabalah, the shell or husks; representations of evil forces in the mystical teachings.

consciousness, and we must therefore examine it carefully and analyze it into the factors of which it consists. Devotion might be defined as love for something higher than ourselves; something that evokes our idealism; which, while we despair of becoming equal to it, yet makes us aspire to become like it; "Beholding as in a glass the glory of the Lord, are changed into the same image from glory to glory." When a stronger emotional content is infused into devotion and it becomes adoration, it carries us across the great gulf fixed between the tangible and the intangible and enables us to apprehend things that eye hath not seen, nor ear heard. It is this Devotion, rising to Adoration, in the Great Work, which initiates us into the Mysteries of the Crucifixion.

The Vice assigned to Tiphareth is Pride, and in this attribution, we have some very true psychology. Pride has its roots in egoism, and as long as we are self-centered, we cannot be made one with all things. In the true selflessness of the Path the soul overflows its boundaries and enters into all things through limitless sympathy and perfect love; but in pride, the soul tries to extend its boundaries till it possesses all things, and it is a very different matter to possess a thing than to being made one with it, wherein it equally possesses us in perfect reciprocity. It is this one-sided arrangement which is the vice of the adept. He must give as well as receive, and he must give himself unreservedly if he would participate in mystical union, which is the fruit of the sacrifice of crucifixion. "Let him who would be the greatest among you be the servant of all," said Our Lord.

The symbols associated with Tiphareth are the lamen; the Rosy Cross; the Calvary Cross; the truncated pyramid; and the cube.

The lamen is the symbol upon the breast of the adept, and indicates the force he represents. An adept performing work in the Sphere of Shemesh, for instance, would wear upon his breast an image of the sun in splendor. A lamen is the magical weapon of Tiphareth; and it therefore becomes necessary to say something concerning the nature of magical weapons, in general, in order that the function of a lamen can be understood.

A magical weapon is some object which is found to be suitable as a vehicle for force of a particular type. For instance, the magical weapon of the Element of Water is a cup or chalice; the magical weapon of the Element of Fire is a lighted lamp. These objects are chosen because their nature is congenial to that of the force to be invoked; or in modern language, because their form suggests the force to the imagination by association of ideas.

Tiphareth is traditionally associated with the breast, both by virtue of the network of nerves which is called the solar plexus, and by its position, when the Tree is built up in the aura. Consequently, the breast jewel of the adept is held to be the focus of the Tiphareth force, whatever operation may be performed.

The actual force, operating in its own sphere, is represented by the magical weapon assigned to it. For instance, an adept performing an operation of the Element of Water would have as his magical weapon the Cup, and with the Cup would make all signs, and upon the Cup would concentrate the force called down by invocation. But upon his breast would be the sigil of the Element of Water, and this would be recognized as representing the spiritual factor in the operation, and as referring to the archangel over that particular kingdom. Unless the adept understands the significance of his lamen, as distinguished from his magical weapon, he is no adept, but a wizard.

The Rosy Cross and the Calvary Cross are both given as symbols of the Sphere of Tiphareth. In order to understand their significance, it is necessary to say something concerning crosses in general, and how they are used in systems of symbolism. Although the cross with which we are most generally familiar is the Calvary Cross, owing to its association with Christianity, there are many other forms of cross, and each has its own significance. The Equal-armed Cross, such as the Red Cross of the army medical service, is called by initiates the Cross of Nature, and represents power in equilibrium. It is to be found at the top of some Keltic crosses, often enclosed in a circle, so that a Keltic cross, actually, consists of a tapering shaft ending in a nature cross, and has no relationship whatever to the Calvary Cross, which is the Cross of Christianity. The tapering shaft of the Keltic cross is, in actual fact, a truncated pyramid, and examples of this type of Keltic cross exist which leave no doubt upon this point whatsoever. Some archaic forms suggest the imposition of the cross and circle upon the conical phallic stone which is so universal an object in primitive worship.

The Swastika is also a nature cross, and is sometimes called the Cross of Thor, or the Hammer of Thor, its form being supposed to indicate the whirling action of his thunderbolts.

The Calvary Cross is the Cross of Sacrifice, and, should properly be colored black. Its shaft should be three times the length of its arms, and the length of each arm, three times its width. Meditation on this cross brings initiation through suffering, sacrifice, and self-abnegation. The Crucifix is, of course, an elaboration of the Calvary Cross.

The circle upon the cross is an initiatory symbol, especially when the cross is raised upon three steps, as it should be in this form. The circle indicates eternal life; also wisdom; and we see a form of it in the emblem of the Theosophical Society, which has for its badge the "serpent that holdeth his tail in his mouth." A Calvary Cross with the circle super-imposed means initiation by the Way of the Cross, and the three steps are the three degrees of illumination. It is this which is the so-called Rosy Cross. The fanciful object with brambles growing over it is not an initiatory symbol at all. The Rose associated with the Cross in Western symbolism is the Rosa Mundi and is a key to the interpretation of the nature forces. On its petals are marked the thirty-two signs of the natural forces; these correspond to the twenty-two letters of the Hebrew alphabet and the Ten Holy Sephiroth; these in their turn are assigned to the Thirty-two Paths of the Tree of Life, and this is the key to the understanding of the Rosa Mundi. The curious scribbles that are called the sigils of the elementary spirits are made by drawing

lines from one to another of the letters of
their names on the Rose.

In the light of this explanation, we are at no
loss to understand the value of the claims of
those organizations which sport a floral
emblem as their symbol. They are on par with
those of the gentleman who demanded of his
haberdasher a public school tie with a bit of
red in it.

The cube is usually said to be assigned to
Tiphareth because it is a six-sided figure, and
six is the number of Tiphareth. But there is
more than this in the symbolism of the cube.
The cube is the simplest form of solid, and as
such is the appropriate symbol of Tiphareth,
in whose sphere is found the first
foreshadowing of form. The symbol of
Malkuth is the double cube, which symbolizes
"As above, so below."

The pyramid symbolizes the perfected man,
broad-based on earth and tapering to unity in
the heavens; in other words, the Ipsissimus.
The truncated pyramid symbolizes the
initiated adept, or Adeptus Minor, who has
passed within the Veil but has not yet
completed his grades. This pyramid, to whose
six sides correspond the six central Sephiroth
which constitute Adam Kadmon, or the
Archetypal Man, is completed by the addition

of the Three Supernals which terminate in the unity of Kether.

The Sixes of the Tarot suits are also assigned to Tiphareth, and in them, the harmonious and balanced nature of this Sephirah shows clearly. The Six of Wands is the Lord of Victory. The Six of Cups, the Lord of Joy. Even the maleficent Suit of Swords is tuned to harmony in this sphere, and the Six of Swords is known as the Lord of Earned Success – that is to say, success achieved after struggle. The Six of Pentacles is Material Success; in other words, power in equilibrium.

CHAPTER 6

The Inverted Fifth Dimension

As I mentioned in the previous chapter, the third dimension takes up a portion of Malkuth. The other portion, which is larger, is occupied by the inverted fifth dimension. This is something that most people have never heard of, let alone understand.

To understand the meaning of the inverted fifth dimension, we must first understand what the fifth dimension is. Basically, it is the upper astral plane and the mental plane. For the full detailed explanation of the fifth dimension, go over the previous chapter.

The fifth dimension is made up of Hod and Netzach in the Tree of Life.

In summary, Netzach is, based on the Yetziratic Text, the path of occult intelligence, because it is the refulgent splendor of the intellectual virtues which are perceived by the eyes of the intellect and the contemplations of faith. The virtue of Netzach is unselfishness and the vice is unchastity and lust.

And Hod is, based on the Yetziratic Text, the
path of absolute or perfect intelligence
because it is the mean of the Primordial,
which has no root by which it can cleave or
rest, save in the hidden places of Gedulah,
from which emanates its proper essence. The
virtue of Hod is truthfulness, and the vice is
falsehood and dishonesty.

So, in this chapter we will discuss the inverted
fifth dimension from three angles. Firstly,
from the angle of it being the inversion of the
correct astral and mental planes. Secondly,
from the summary of Netzach. Thirdly, from
the summary of Hod. Let's begin.

If we look at the inversion of the upper astral
and mental planes, we can already begin to see
why the illusion exists, and why it needs to
exist. The mental plane is the plane of
intelligence. Not the regular kind of
intelligence, but the occult intelligence
(Netzach). The occult intelligence is the
knowledge of the intelligible world, the
wisdom of the ages and true knowledge.
Malkuth, which is where we are currently, is
mainly in the inverted fifth dimension, which
means that the sphere is influenced by the
opposite of the occult intelligence. That is,
ignorance of those things. There is no proper
understanding, if any at all, of the true
knowledge, of the ancient wisdom. This is

exactly why we said in previous sections of
this book, that we live in an age of opinions.
This will become even more apparent as we
discuss it from the standpoint of Netzach.

It says in the Yetziratic Texts about Netzach,
"the path of occult intelligence, because it is
the refulgent splendor of the intellectual
virtues *which are perceived by the eyes of the intellect
and the contemplations of faith.*"

Notice the section in italics. The occult
intelligence being discussed here is perceived
by the eyes of the intellect, and the
contemplations of faith. This tells us two
important things.

One, that the eyes of the intellect spoken of
here is the same as the dual mechanisms of
the eye which we mentioned earlier. One
mechanism showing us illusion, and the other
showing us reality. Obviously, the mechanism
referred to here, about Netzach, is about
reality. The second point here, is that along
with the eyes of intellect, we need the
contemplations of faith. This points to the
fact that we must have the gnosis gained from
at one point being in the state of Pistis,
combined with the eyes of the intellect, to
gain the occult intelligence. This is why we
stressed the point earlier about the necessity
of passing successfully through all the stages

of consciousness and not disregarding religion as the mass mind does nowadays.

In addition to that, we can see the virtue and vice of Netzach is unselfishness and lust/unchastity, respectively. This also confirms our points from the chapters on the Kundalini and the Sublimation of the Mind, on the need for the Kundalini energy to be flowing in the correct direction, and for the man not to be controlled by the lower nature, to reveal the knowledge. That's why we called the Kundalini the Axis of Understanding.

To further clarify this point, we must understand that every sphere of the Tree of Life can express itself in a positive or negative manifestation. The vice of the sphere denotes the negative attribute. So, if lust and unchastity are the vices, then we can say that those attributes manifest when it is inverted. This is what is happening; emanating from Netzach, in the inverted fifth dimension.

Next, let's move on to Hod. According to the Yetziratic Texts, it says, "the path of absolute or perfect intelligence because it is the mean of the Primordial, which has no root by which it can cleave or rest, *save in the hidden places of Gedulah, from which emanates its proper essence.*"

Notice the section in italics. The perfect
intelligence has its root in the hidden places of
Gedulah, from which emanates its proper
essence. This elucidates an important point
regarding Noesis and the meaning of it.

Noesis, as we now know, means clear vision
and it is the highest plane of consciousness. It
is also at the apex of the triangle. Being at the
apex indicates that it has no duality.
Everything is coming from one. From
singularity. Hod states that the perfect
intelligence (which we know to be the ability
to see reality), has its roots in Gedulah.
Gedulah means the greatness, magnificence,
or glory. We attribute that to the one, the
source of All Good. And further, Hod, ends
with saying that Gedulah is where it emanates
its proper essence. This is a complete
confirmation about the location of Noesis on
the triangle, the reason for it being at the
apex, and the concept that everything stems
from good. In addition to that, it confirms the
concept that once clear vision is gained, we
see the reality in totality, and it all comes from
the same place. Finally, this indicates and
confirms that all duality is false.

The texts about Hod also state that
truthfulness is the virtue and falsity, and
dishonesty are the vice. Therefore, in the
inverted fifth dimension, we can understand

there to be falsity and dishonesty about everything regarding the true spiritual wisdom. And we have spoken along the same lines all throughout this book.

So, we must understand that in Malkuth, the illusion is created by the inversion of the fifth dimension. It covers the majority of the sphere. Only when the illusion is broken through and we see the full reality, do we venture into the actual third dimension. This fact tells us that we haven't even seen the real third dimension. Yet, people living in Eikasia all over the world are preparing to move into the fifth dimension. That is all part of the illusion.

CHAPTER 7

Key 12, The Hanged Man

The Hanged Man is one of the most important Keys of the Tarot to understand in relation to uncovering the illusion of the world.

First, let's start of by noting the following:

The Qabalistic Intelligence corresponding to Key 12: Stable Intelligence

The Power corresponding to Key 12: The Law of Reversal

The Color corresponding to Key 12: Blue

We will start this section by defining the occult Law of Reversal.

The Law of Reversal: to reverse the conditions of misery, disease, and failure, and substitute them their opposites of health, happiness, and success, it is necessary to think, speak, and act in ways which are the reverse of the way most persons think, speak and act.

Now let us understand that the way most persons think, speak and act is another way of saying public opinion (and action). Key 12 states that we must reverse this; reverse public opinion. We mentioned this in a prior chapter. This is reversing doxa, which requires a Noetic way of thinking. This is living in the Intelligible World. Key 12 is literally stating to do things opposite to doxa.

Key 12 also has to do with the Hebrew letter Mem, which means water. Why water? Water reverses everything. It reflects, and in the reflection, it is reversed. We are speaking of fixed water here. This water is the heavenly water. It is the seed. And this is connected to the proper flow of Kundalini energy. The water is an electro-magnetic substance. It is also the astral fluid.

The astral fluid is what shapes everything. The manipulation of astral fluid manipulates the matter around the person. From the densest matter to the lightest, it is all built by the astral fluid. When one wants to change their surroundings, they must manipulate the substance.

The problem with most is that they accept the appearances of what things are. Do not accept the appearances of anything as they are not real. Appearances are not real and this is

Figure 4 Key 12 The Hanged Man

something that must be totally understood on the spiritual path.

The senses are what interpret the appearances of things. But the wise man knoweth that his senses do not report accurate things to him. Therefore, he does not accept the appearances. Remember always that the senses do not report accurately to the person. This is of primary importance.

The pouring of the subconscious through action of the consciousness is the key here.

The Hanged Man is also the suspended man. The man has suspended himself (and his senses). He understands about the inaccurate reporting done by the senses and has thus suspended himself. With the suspension of yourself comes the reversal.

Only the truly wise follow the Law of Reversal. This law is the exact opposite of public opinion or doxa. What the wise man values, is viewed as worthless by the average man.

There should be effected a reversal of the superficial, deluded interpretation of the universe which holds the ordinary human being in bondage. This is the way to see the illusion. Once the suspension occurs, once the person knows factually that their senses are reporting inaccuracies, the revelation of truth begins.

Key 12 represents absolute freedom. But to the average man, it looks like bondage and suffering. Think about it. An average man sees this Tarot card and immediately what comes to his mind? He views the Hanged Man as someone suffering because he is tied up and hanging upside down. This is completely wrong, isn't it? Indeed, it is wrong and this represents the situation of doxa versus episteme.

The water represented here is a metaphysical water, seen in so many occult texts.

Only one who has experienced a reversal in consciousness can truly understand what the water is. Alchemists call it the water of the wise.

The water is the Root of Nature and/or Mother Deep.

The subconsciousness is actually the substance of every form in the universe. The universal subconsciousness is also your personal subconsciousness. This means that you have the ability to govern the creative powers of this substance.

One thing which makes all forms of mental and occult practice seem difficult is the supposition that what we have to do demands an exertion of some intangible mental power, which must be pitted against the inertia of a very tangible physical reality. We think that we don't have control over the dense "matter" surrounding us, not knowing that it is not dense, and it is in fact, the same substance within us.

The wise man is not deceived by the surface appearances. He understands that everything is really forms of energy made up of drops of the water of the alchemists.

He realizes he can change his conditions by changing his thinking.

Again, he knows that the senses are not accurately reporting to him, and he knows that there is no difference between the energy which takes form as thought and the energy which takes form as a diamond, or any other physical object.

The occult teaching about water as a substance is precisely the same as the scientific conception of the electrical constitution of matter, and this enable him to effect a reversal in his environment.

By this reversal, he is able to free his mind from the subjection to appearances.

So, there are several things to learn and understand from this Tarot Key.

Firstly, we must understand that the Law of Reversal is one of the primary things to grasp properly when trying to reveal the illusion of the world. The doxa of the mass mind is something that has to be reversed. This can only happen when we understand fully the inaccuracy of the senses and what they are reporting to us.

We should look at the inaccuracy of the senses as something that is to be expected, not something unusual. This is so because the human body itself only belongs to this sphere, the sphere of Malkuth. It is the final condensation of the spirit and thus the least pure from the actual essence of our being. If the body is the final condensation, how can the receiving instruments of it be accurate? They cannot.

Man has relied on his senses for everything. To interact with the illusory world, we must rely on the senses. But to interact with the invisible, intelligible world, man must detach from the senses and rely on the knowledge which he possesses to accurately debunk the inaccuracy of the senses. This is the main concept being portrayed in the Hanged Man Key.

If we take a close look at the image of the Hanged Man, we see the man's head in a river or stream valley. This means that his head is where there would be water. Again, we see the reference to the heavenly waters. The water, as mentioned earlier, is something that reverses the image, or the reality in this case. If the man's head is in the water, allegorically, we can see that he is reversing what is already reversed. Thus, he is bringing it to its actuality, its reality.

We can also see the number four being made by the position of the Hanged Man. The number four in Hebrew is daleth and means door. The door being referred to here is the door which, once opened, allows you to exit from illusion and enter into the reality of Noesis.

In the next chapter we will discuss the appearances in greater detail as it pertains directly to Key 15, The Devil.

CHAPTER 8

Key 15, The Devil

N ow that we have an understanding of Key 12, The Hanged Man, in relation to the illusion, let's talk about appearances and Key 15, The Devil.

The esoteric meaning of Key 15 is the *absence of the equilibrating power*. What equilibrating power? That is, the power to find balance between the world of objective appearances, through which we gain knowledge, and the subjective world of consciousness, through which we gain knowledge.

The eye is associated with Key 15 and the Hebrew word for eye is *ayin*. Ayin also means vision, outward show, superficial appearances, and fountain.

Therefore, we are to understand that the eye can either be the deceiver or the revealer. It can deceive us by seeing the illusion or it can reveal to us by looking beyond the illusion to reality.

As we see in the Great Seal of the United States of America, the eye on the top of the pyramid has a great significance not understood by the mass mind. As the doxa relating to this is erroneous, the real meaning can teach us a great deal.

We mentioned one of the meanings of ayin is the fountain. We are to understand here that God is the fountain of manifestation in this world. He is the source of all appearances. By placing the eye on top of the pyramid, we must know that our vision is what shapes our reality and the world. This is the reason why the mass mind faces fear and worry about the future, and the realized man worries not. If we think of the pyramid as representing the triangle of consciousness, we can understand that once a person reaches the state of Noesis, they will clearly understand the meaning of the eye that sits there. The eye can either be the source of illusion or the reality. The consciousness is the mediator. The consciousness dictates what the eye interprets.

Think of a mirage in the desert. When seen from afar, we are certain there is water there. Our eyes are deceiving us due to the lack of knowledge we have. Once we explore the desert and realize there is no water, the next time we see the mirage, we will not be deceived. Think of it like this. When we see the mirage for the first time, we believe our imagination (Eikasia) of the water. Once we have been there and back, we see it again with

Figure 5 Key 15, The Devil

clear vision (Noesis) and know it is not there. We have the same eyes, but we have an elevated consciousness regarding the mirage.

The word Devil comes from the Greek word *Diabolos,* which means the slanderer. The primary deception of the Devil is the fundamental error from where all other falsehoods proceed. This is the error of supposing that a reality called matter is opposed to another called spirit.

Matter in Sanskrit is called maya. Another meaning for maya, as mentioned in earlier pages, is illusion.

Matter, in reality, is the appearance of spirit. Anytime we try to separate the two, there is error. The two are the same. They are not in opposition to each other.

So, if we think about this in the context of the dialectic, we can see that what causes our error in thinking at all levels of consciousness below Noesis, is a result of separating matter from spirit. And this is clearly represented in the Noetic Triangle. Eikasia is located at the base which has two ends (representing the duality of thinking), and Noesis is located at the apex of the triangle (which is one singular point). The Singular point of Noesis denotes

here the understanding that matter and spirit
are one.

Think about the vast majority of the world
and their viewpoint on the Devil. They
imagine the Devil to be the opposite of God.
They imagine the Devil to be the enemy of
God. This is the dialectic of Eikasia and Pistis.

The people in Eikasia imagine this to be the
case based on the impressions they have
received, both consciously and
subconsciously. There is no evidence of
anything they imagine.

The very few people who are in Pistis believe
this to be the case based on their incorrect
understanding of the religions. It is in fact an
incorrect understanding, not an incorrect
presentation. All the religions of the world
teach what I am stating here, in allegory.

So, we can see that the Noetic vision of the
Devil is something far different from the
doxa.

Further, the Devil represents the appearance
of everything. And this is what creates
bondage. When we become attached to
appearances, it is called bondage. This
concept is represented in the Tarot image of
the man and woman chained to the box the

Devil is sitting on. This is the reason the Devil is known as the Lord of this world. Because it is He who has given us the illusion. But it is also important to know that it is He who is also God. They are one in the same.

The only way to release ourselves from those chains is to dis-attach from the appearances (matter) and understand the spirit that it is cloaking. In order to do this, we must understand a couple of important things. Firstly, that the senses are what focus on and attach us to appearances. This is why we mentioned earlier in the book that we must know that our senses are not giving us accurate impressions. If we are to know that the appearances are cloaking the spirit, we must only use our spirit to understand it. The second point to understand is in connection with the previous statement. To use the spirit to connect to everything, we must begin to consciously not become attached to anything in the world. We must do this for an extended period, consciously, for it to become engrained in our minds and override the plethora of impressions we have received throughout our life thus far. This is the first step to climbing the ladder of the evolution of consciousness.

The Allegory of the Mirage

Let's discuss the allegory of the mirage as it tells us how the mind works at different levels of consciousness.

Premise: *A man, traveling in the desert, thirsty.*

The man whose consciousness is in Eikasia looks ahead and sees a beautiful mirage in the distance. He continues walking towards it to satisfy his thirst. As he continues walking, after some time, he believes that there is water there and has faith that his thirst will be quenched when he reaches the sparkling water, so he continues on. Even if he gets tired, he may stop, but his faith, helps him continue on. After walking for miles, his brain begins thinking, "I have been walking forever and it is still in the distance. It doesn't seem that I will ever get there. Also, what is the probability that there is water like that in this barren desert?" He begins to question if the water is actually there, based on the fact that he is in the middle of the desert. His logic says there can be no water. After walking to the giant sand dune, which he saw at the start of his journey that looked small, he realizes there is no water. There never was. It was just an illusion. Now he knows the truth.

Weeks later, he arrives at the same point in the desert. This time, with a friend. His friend is very thirsty and looks ahead and sees the mirage. He tells his friend that there is no water there. That it is just an illusion. His friend, extremely thirsty, disregards what he just told him and begins walking.

This is the story of a man with self-knowledge and a man without. And this is the story of the world.

CHAPTER 9

Key 21, The World

The World is the final card of the Tarot Keys (Major Arcana) and represents the man who has cosmic consciousness based on first-hand knowledge and experience of his identity with the One. This is the level of Noesis.

There is an intimate connection between Key 7, The Chariot, and Key 21, The World.

Saturn, the great Teacher and Lord, is attributed to Key 21 and is also the 7th planet known to the ancients.

In regard to Key 7, the great theosophical text, The Light on the Path, states, "Stand aside in the coming battle, and though thou fightest, be no thou the warrior. Look for the warrior and let him fight in thee. Take his orders for the battle and obey them. Obey him not as though he were a general, but as though he were thyself, and his spoken word were the utterance of thy secret desires…"

The entire quest starting in Eikasia and culminating in Noesis is about yourself. It is about knowing yourself and understanding yourself, completely.

The Egyptian letter Tau is a letter corresponding to Key 21. The symbol of Tau was a cross. This symbol, as spoken of in Ezekial 9:4 was a symbol of eternal life, also a final seal in the completion of the Great Work. All are references to the level of Noesis.

We can see from the Tarot image of Key 21, that the person is holding two rods, one in each hand. The being is in perfect balance and has found equilibrium. The zodiacal signs of the cardinal signs are around. The wreath around the being indicates that cosmic consciousness is not part of natural evolution spontaneously. This means that an active work must be performed to achieve it.

The person understands that the proportion in which the lesser part is to the greater part as the greater part is to the whole. "Nature, the lesser part, is to Man, the greater part, as Man is to the whole."

In esoteric Tarot teachings, one of the main points taught is that the person who has achieved The World, understands that the mechanistic appearance assumed by natural phenomena veils their true character. This

Figure 6 Key 21, The World

clearly indicates the connection to what we discussed about The Devil, Key 15.

Everything is held in balance by necessity. And the person who attains The World or Noesis understands this perfectly.

This is all we will say for the sake of this text on Key 21, The World.

CHAPTER 10

The Negative Existence

The esotericist, when endeavoring to formulate his philosophy for communication to others, is confronted by the fact that his knowledge of the higher forms of existence is obtained by a process other than thought; and this process only commences when thought is left behind. Consequently, it is only in that region of consciousness which transcends thought that the highest form of transcendental ideas is known and understood; and it is only to those who are able to use this aspect of consciousness that he can communicate his ideas in their original form. When he wants to communicate these ideas to those who have had no experience of this mode of consciousness, he must either crystallize them into form or fail to convey any adequate impression. Mystics have used every imaginable simile in the endeavor to convey their impressions; philosophers have lost themselves in a maze of words; and all to no purpose so far as the unilluminated soul is concerned ☺. The Qabalists, however, use another method. They do not try to explain to the mind that which the mind is not equipped to deal with; they give it a series of symbols to meditate upon, and these enable it to build the stairway of realization step by step, and to climb where it cannot fly. The mind can no more grasp transcendent philosophy than the eye can see music.

The Tree of Life, as cannot too often be emphasized, is not so much a system, as a method; those who formulated it realized the important truth that in order to obtain clarity of vision one must circumscribe the field of vision. Most Philosophers founded their systems upon the Absolute; but this is a shifting foundation, for the human mind can neither define nor grasp the Absolute. Some others try to use a negation for their foundation, declaring that the Absolute is, and must ever be, unknowable. The Qabalists do neither of these things.

They content themselves with saying that the Absolute is unknown to the state of consciousness which is normal to human beings.

For the purposes of their system, therefore, they draw a veil at a certain point in manifestation, not because there is nothing there, but because the mind, as such, must stop there. When the human mind has been brought to its highest stage of development, and consciousness can detach itself - and, as it

were, stand upon its own shoulders, we may
be able to penetrate the Veils of Negative
Existence, as they are called. But for all
practical purposes we can understand the
nature of the cosmos if we are content to
accept the Veils as philosophical conventions,
and realize that they correspond to human
limitations, not to cosmic conditions. The
origin of things is inexplicable in terms of our
philosophy. However far we push our
inquiries back into origins in the world of
manifestation, we find a preceding existence.
It is only when we are content to draw the
Veil of Negative Existence across the path
which leads back to beginnings that we get a
background against which a First Cause
becomes visible. And this First Cause is not a
rootless origin, but a First Appearance on the
Plane of Manifestation. Thus far, and no
farther, can the mind go back; but we must
always remember that different minds go back
different distances, and that for some the Veil
is drawn in one place, and for others in
another. The ignorant man goes no further
than the concept of God as an old man with a
long white beard who sat on a golden throne
and gave orders for creation. The scientist will
go back a little further before he is compelled
to draw a veil called the ether; and the
philosopher will go back yet further before he
draws a veil called the Absolute; but the
initiate will go back furthest of all because he

has learnt to do his thinking in symbols, and symbols are to the mind what tools are to the hand-an extended application of its powers.

The Qabalist takes for his starting-point Kether, the Crown, the first Sephirah - which he symbolizes by the figure One, Unity, and by the Point within the Circle. From this he traces backwards the three Veils of Negative Existence. This is quite a different matter from starting at the Absolute and trying to work forwards into evolution. It may not yield immediately accurate and complete knowledge of the origin of all things, but it enables the mind to make a start; and unless we can make a start, we have no hope of a finish.

The Qabalist, then, starts where he can-at the first point that is within the reach of finite consciousness. Kether is equated with the most transcendent form of God that we can conceive, Whose name is Eheieh, translated in the Authorized Version of the Bible as "I am," or, more explicitly, the Self-Existing One, Pure Being.

But these words are words and nothing more unless they convey an impression to the mind, and in themselves they cannot do that. They must be related to other ideas before they have any significance. We only begin to understand Kether, when we study Chokmah,

the Second Sephirah, its emanation; it is only
when we see the full unfoldment of the Ten
Sephiroth that we are ready to approach
Kether, and then we approach it with the data
that gives us the key to its nature. In working
with the Tree, it is wisest to keep on going
over it, rather than to concentrate upon a
single point until it is mastered, for one thing
explains another, and it is out of the
perception of the relationships between the
different symbols, that enlightenment arises.
Again, we say, the Tree is a method of using
the mind, not a system of knowledge.

But at the moment, we are not engaged in the
study of the Emanations, but of origins, so far
as the human mind may hope to penetrate
them; and paradoxical as it may appear, we
shall penetrate further when we draw the
Veils across them, than when we try to pierce
the darkness. We will, then, sum up the
position of Kether in one sentence, a sentence
that can have but little significance for the
student approaching the subject for the first
time, but which must be borne in mind, for its
significance will begin to dawn presently. In
so doing, we are adhering to the ancient
esoteric tradition of giving the student a
symbol to incubate till it hatches in his mind,
rather than explicit instruction which would
convey nothing to him.

The seed-sentence then, which we cast into the subconscious mind of the reader, is this: "Kether is the Malkuth of the Unmanifest." Mathers says (op. cit.): "The limitless ocean of negative light does not proceed from a center, for it is centerless, but it concentrates a center, which is the number One of the manifested Sephiroth, Kether, the Crown, the First Sephirah."

These words in themselves contain contradictions and unthinkable things; negative light is simply a way of saying that the thing described, though having certain qualities in common with light, is nevertheless not light as we know it. This tells us very little about that which it is intended to describe. We are told not to make the mistake of thinking of it as light, but we are not told how to think of it as it really is, and for the very good reason that the mind is not equipped with any images under which to represent it and must, therefore, let it alone till growth takes place. Nevertheless, although these words do not tell us all that we would like to know, they convey certain images to imagination; these sink into the subconscious mind which are related to them. Thus, knowledge grows from more to more when the Qabalistic method is given its practical application as the Yoga of the West.

The Qabalists recognize four planes of
manifestation, and three planes of
unmanifestation, or Negative Existence. The
first of these is called AIN, Negativity; the
second, AIN SOPH, the Limitless; the third,
AIN SOPH AUR, the Limitless Light. It is
out of this last, that Kether is concentrated.
These three terms are called the three Veils of
Negative Existence - depending back from
Kether; in other words, they are the algebraic
symbols that enable us to think of that which
transcends thought, and which at the same
time hide that which they represent; they are
the masks of transcendent realities. If we
think of the states of negative existence in
terms of anything that we know, we shall err,
for whatever else they may be, they cannot be
that, being unmanifest. The expression
"Veils," therefore, teaches us to use these
ideas as counters, of no value in themselves,
but useful to us in our calculations. This is the
true use of all symbols; they veil that which
they represent until we can reduce them to
terms we can comprehend; nevertheless they
enable us to use in our calculations ideas
which would otherwise be unthinkable.

And as the essence of the Tree lies in the fact
that it causes its symbols to elucidate one
another by means of their relative positions,
these Veils serve as the scaffolding of
thought, enabling us to take our bearings in

regions as yet uncharted. Such Veils, or non-concrete symbols, are, however, of no value to us unless one side of the Veil abuts upon known country. The Veils, in fact, while they conceal that which they represent, enable us to see clearly that to which they form a background. This is their function, and the only reason they are referred to. It is only by reason of our infirmities that we need to have these unresolvable symbols presented to us, and the mind disciplined in esoteric philosophy soon learns to work within these limitations and accept as a painted veil the symbol of that which lies beyond its ken. This way lies the unfoldment of wisdom, for the mind grows with what it feeds upon, and one of these days, when we have climbed to Kether, we may hope to stretch out our hands and rend the Veil and look through into the Limitless Light. The esotericist does not limit himself by declaring the Unknown to be the Unknowable, for he is above all things an evolutionist, and knows that that which we cannot compass today we may achieve tomorrow of cosmic time. He knows, too, that evolutionary time is an individual matter upon the inner planes, and is measured, not regulated, by the revolution of the earth upon its axis.

These three Veils - AIN, Negativity; AIN SOPH, the Limitless; and AIN SOPH AUR,

the Limitless Light - though we cannot hope
to understand them, nevertheless suggest to
our minds certain ideas. Negativity implies
Being or existence of a nature which we
cannot comprehend. We cannot conceive of a
thing which is, and yet is not; therefore, we
must conceive of a form of being of which we
have never had any conscious experience; a
form of being which, according to our
concepts of existence, does not exist, and yet,
if one may express it so, exists according to its
own idea of existence. In the words of a very
wise man: There are more things in heaven
and earth than are dreamt of in our
philosophy.

But although we say that Negative Existence
is outside the range of our realization, it does
not mean that we are outside the range of its
influence. If this were so, we could dismiss it
as non-existent so far as we are concerned,
and our interest in it would be at an end. On
the contrary, although we have not direct
access to its being, all that we know as existing
has its roots in this Negative Existence, so
that, although we cannot know it directly, we
have experience of it at one remove. That is
to say, although we cannot know its nature,
we know its effects, in the same way as we are
ignorant of the nature of electricity yet are
able to turn it to good account in our lives,
and from our experience of its effects we are

able to come to certain conclusions concerning some, at least, of the qualities it must possess. Those who have penetrated furthest into the Unseen have given us symbolic descriptions by means of which we may turn our minds in the direction of the Absolute, even if we cannot reach it. They have spoken of Negative Existence as Light: "Ain Soph Aur, the Limitless Light." They have spoken of the First Manifest as Sound: "In the beginning was the Word." I remember once hearing a man, who was an adept if ever there was one, say, "If you want to know what God is, I can tell you in one word: God is pressure." And immediately an image leapt to my mind and a realization followed. I could conceive the outflowing of life through every channel of existence. I felt that a genuine realization of the nature of God had been conveyed to me. And yet, if one were to analyze the words, there was nothing in them; nevertheless they had the power to convey an image, a symbol, to the mind, and the mind, working upon it in the realm of intuition beyond the sphere of reason, achieved a realization, even if that realization could only be reduced to the sphere of concrete thought as an image.

We must clearly realize that in these highly abstract regions the mind can use nothing but symbols; but these symbols have the power to

convey realizations to minds that know how
to use them; these symbols are the seeds of
thought whence understanding arises, even if
we are not able to expand the symbol itself
into a concrete realization.

Little by little, like a rising tide, realization is
concreting the Abstract, assimilating and
expressing in terms of its own nature things
which belong to another sphere; and we shall
make a great mistake if we try to prove with
Herbert Spencer that because a thing is
unknown by any capacity of the mind, we at
present possess, that it must forever be
Unknowable. Time is not only increasing our
knowledge, but evolution is increasing our
capacity and initiation, which is the forcing-
house of evolution, bringing faculties to birth
out of due season, brings the consciousness of
the adept within reach of vast apprehensions
which are as yet below the horizon of the
human mind. These ideas, though clearly
apprehended by himself after another mode
of consciousness, cannot be conveyed by him
to anyone who does not share this mode of
consciousness. He can only put them forth in
symbolic form; but any mind that has in any
way had experience of this wider mode of
functioning will be able to lay hold on these
ideas on their own plane, although it may be
unable to translate them into the sphere of
conscious thought. In this way, therefore, in

the literature of esoteric science there are
scattered seed-ideas such as "God is pressure"
and "Kether is the Malkuth of Negative
Existence." These images, whose content
does not belong to our sphere at all, are as the
male germs of thought which fecundate the
ova of concrete realization. In themselves they
are incapable of maintaining more than the
fugitive existence in consciousness as a flash
of realization, but without them the ova of
philosophical thought will be infertile.
Impregnated by them, however, though their
substance is absorbed and lost in the very act
of impregnation, growth takes place within
the formless germ of thought, and ultimately,
after due gestation beyond the threshold of
consciousness, the mind gives birth to an idea.

If we want to get the best out of our minds,
we must learn to allow for this period of
latency, this impregnation of our minds by
something outside our plane of existence, and
its gestation beyond the threshold of
consciousness. The invocations of an
initiation ceremony are designed to call down
this impregnating influence upon the
consciousness of the candidate. Hence it is
that the Paths of the Tree, which are the
stages of illumination of the soul, are
intimately associated with the symbolism of
initiation ceremonies.

CHAPTER 11

The Right and Left Hand Paths

In occult and esoteric literature, we see that the content is usually divided into two sections. These two sections represent the two "paths" that have been frequently mentioned as spiritual paths. They are the right-hand path and the left-hand path. In the following paragraphs, we will provide a summary of what each path means and then compare the two.

The Right Hand Path

The right-hand path has been presented as being synonymous with a benevolent path, with the goal being union with "God" or the Divine. In the Western Occult Tradition, the right-hand path is the benevolent, "white" magical path.

Let's talk about the Eastern view first. Union with the divine is the goal. It means that the aspirant will be joined with (yoga) or merge with the divine spirit. Usually, we see right hand path practitioners becoming monks in the East.

<u>The Left Hand Path</u>

The left-hand path has been represented as being associated with "black" magic, where the aspirant is self-serving and not interested in merging with God, and in some cases, not even accepting God as the highest, and seeking to go higher.

In the Eastern Tradition, it is known as Vamamarga[44], and means opposing the societal norms and using those opposing ideals to perform sadhana[45] and achieve spiritual objectives.

Both popular opinions are essentially erroneous. This is because, while there are two paths, they do not delineate the summaries usually given.

The Right-Hand Path claims to be a benevolent type of ceremonial magic, from a Western Tradition standpoint. If we analyze this correctly, we will understand that any union with a divine being would prevent the use of any type of ceremonial magic (or any other kind), to reach an objective. The definition of magic alone would defy the argument. Magic is the use of will, and will is

---

[44] A tantric term meaning "left-hand" path used to describe a particular mode of worship or sadhana.
[45] An ego transcending spiritual practice.

an independent, individual thing, not part of natural living. To merge with a divine being, would mean to simply follow the course of life (lives) and then "end up" where that diving being wanted you to. But the idea that one could change the course of their life by performing ceremonial magic practices, defies that way of living categorically.

In addition, from an Eastern standpoint, the monk, who is a great example of a supposed right hand path practitioner, is a point of contention. The reason for this, is because the monk's daily activities and austerities are so immense and grueling, that it could hardly be described using the traditional definition of the path.

Monks are known for undergoing some of the most intense austerities, and the mere fact that they already live in an anti-societal way, better fits the description given to the left hand.

The left-hand path also has its issues with the common explanation. To assume that it is "black" magic, without understanding it, is clearly an Eikasia-based way of thinking. The left-hand path has mainly become known as such due to its unconventional methods of achieving spiritual goals. But, again, so has the monk.

So, we can say that the doxa of these two paths is erroneous.

A noetic thinker would explain the two paths as simply the same. The paths are the same, but the goals are different. The goal of the right-hand path being merging with the divine, and the goal of the left-hand path being to surpass the divine. Their methods are essentially the same.

For example, let us use the story of Jesus as an example. The mass mind will assume, due to the religious connotations, that Jesus' life was a right-hand path example. However, if we have a proper understanding of the two, and take a closer look, we may see things differently. The life of Jesus, and the hardships he had to go through, culminating in the crucifixion, all fit perfectly into the description of the "unorthodox" methods used to attain spiritual advancement. Basically, there is no "benevolent" method of reaching spiritual advancement. Benevolent, in the case of these definitions has been incorrectly used to assume something easier. And this is not true. There is no benevolence without total understanding.

Noesis will tell us that, there are not two paths, but only one. This is so for multiple reasons, two of which I will discuss here.

The first reason is that all spiritual advancement happens only with harsh, intense, and often painful experiences which teach us and give us the gnosis required to progress. If you view the monk, who has given up the world, and dedicated his life to sadhana and austerities as easy, you are mistaken. So, the method of the path is always the same.

The correlation of a particular path to a form of magic is also erroneous. A supposed right hand path practitioner is still capable of performing selfish works of magic (what doxa would consider black magic) and vice versa for the left-hand path practitioner.

Aside from this, the second reason is that we must understand where we are in our evolution to accurately "choose" a path.

Can a person, born into sin and from sin, really choose a right-hand path, if there was one to choose? According to popular definitions of the right-hand path, it assumes that you live in perfection. It requires no error in judgment and it requires this to be maintained from day one. Who, on this Earth, has lived this way. If we simply look at the Ten Commandments, as an example, we see that there is no one who has not violated at least one of these laws. If that violation has occurred, that path, if it were available to choose, is not available to you. You would be damned, from a religious point of view.

So, this leaves only one path available to people on the Earth. A path of self-acknowledgement and fixing all issues of our psychology. A path of mastering all our demons. And who is the master of demons? Esoterically, the Devil, is the master of the demons. The Devil is also the master of illusions. When we master our demons and the illusion, we become masters. This is the path. The only path.

No student will ever make any progress in spiritual development who flits from system to system; first using some New Thought affirmations, then some Yoga breathing exercises and meditation-postures, and following these by an attempt at the mystical methods of prayer. Each of these systems has its value, but that value can only be realized if the system is carried out in its entirety. They are the calisthenics of consciousness, and aim at gradually developing the powers of the mind. The value does not lie in the prescribed exercises as ends in themselves, but in the powers that will be developed if they are persevered with. If we intend to take our occult studies seriously and make of them anything more than desultory light reading, we must choose our system and carry it out faithfully until we arrive, if not at its ultimate goal, at any rate, at definite practical results and a permanent enhancement of consciousness. After this has been achieved, we may, not without advantage, experiment with the methods that have been developed upon other Paths, and build up an eclectic technique and philosophy therefrom; but the student who sets out to be an eclectic before he has made himself an expert will never be anything more than a dabbler.

Whoever has any practical experience of the different methods of spiritual development knows that the method must fit the temperament, and that it must also be adapted to the grade of development of the student. Westerners, especially such, as who prefer the occult to the mystic Path, often come seeking initiation at a stage of spiritual development which an Eastern guru would consider exceedingly immature.

Any method that is to be available for the West must have in its lower grades a technique which can be used as a stepping-stone by these undeveloped students; to ask them to rise immediately to metaphysical heights is useless in the case of the great majority, and prevents a start from being made.

For a system of spiritual development to be applicable in the West, it must fulfil certain well-defined requirements. To begin with, its elementary technique must be such that it is readily grasped by minds that have in them nothing of the mystic. Secondly, the forces it brings to bear to stimulate the development of the higher aspects of consciousness, must be sufficiently powerful and concentrated to penetrate the relatively dense vehicles of the average Westerner, who makes nothing whatever of subtle vibrations. Thirdly, as few Europeans, following a racial dharma of material development, have either the opportunity, or the inclination, to lead the life of a recluse, the forces employed must be handled in such a way that they can be made available during the brief periods that the modern man or woman can, at the commencement of the Path, snatch from their daily avocations to give to the pursuit. They must, that is to say, be handled by a technique which enables them to be readily concentrated and equally readily dispersed, because it is not possible to maintain these high psychic tensions while living the hard-driving life of the citizen of a European or Western city. Experience proves with unfailing regularity that the methods of psychic development which are effectual and satisfactory for the recluse produce neurotic conditions and breakdowns in the person who pursues them while compelled to endure the strain of modern life.

So much the worse for modern life, some may say, and adduce this undeniable fact as an argument for modifying our Western ways of living. Far be it from me to maintain that our civilization is perfect, or that wisdom originated and will die with us, but it appears to me that if our karma (or destiny) has caused us to be incarnated in a body of a certain racial type and temperament, it may be concluded that that is the discipline and experience which the Lords of Karma consider we need in this incarnation, and that we shall not advance the cause of our evolution by avoiding or evading it. I have seen so many attempts at spiritual development that were simply evasions of life's problems, that I am suspicious of any system which involves a breach with the group-soul of the race. Nor am I impressed by a dedication to the higher life which manifests itself by peculiarities of clothing and bearing and by the manner of cutting, or omitting to cut, the hair. True spirituality never advertises itself.

The racial dharma of the West is the conquest of dense matter. If this were realized, it would explain many problems in the relationships of West and East. In order that we may conquer dense matter and develop the concrete mind we are endowed by our racial heritage with a particular type of physical body and nervous system, just as other races, are endowed with other types.

It is injudicious to apply to one type of psycho-physical make-up the developing methods adapted to another; they will either fail to produce adequate results, or produce unforeseen and possibly undesirable results. To say this is not to condemn the Eastern methods, nor decry the Western constitution, which is as God made it, but to reaffirm the old adage that one man's meat is another man's poison.

The dharma of the West differs from that of the East; is it therefore desirable to try and implant Eastern ideals in a Westerner? Withdrawal from the earth-plane is not his line of progress. The normal, healthy Westerner has no desire to escape from life, his urge is to conquer it and reduce it to order and harmony. It is only the pathological types who long to "cease upon the midnight with no pain," to be free from the wheel of birth

and death; the normal Western temperament
demands "life, more life."

It is this concentration of life-force that the
Western occultist seeks in his operations.
He does not try to escape from matter into
spirit, leaving an unconquered country behind
him to get on as best it may; he wants to bring
the Godhead down into manhood and
make Divine Law prevail even in the
Kingdom of the Shades. This is the root-
motive for the acquisition of occult powers
upon the Right-hand Path and explains why
initiates do not abandon all for the mystic
Divine Union, but cultivate a White Magic.

It is this White Magic, which consists in the
application of occult powers to spiritual
ends, by means of which a large proportion of
the training and development of the
Western aspirant is carried out. I have seen
something of a good many different systems,
and in my opinion the person who tries to
dispense with ceremonial is working at a great
disadvantage. Development by meditation
alone is a slow process in the West, because
the mind-stuff upon which it has to work, and
the mental atmosphere in which the work
has to be done, are very resistant. The only
purely meditative school of Western Yoga is
that of the Quakers, and I think that they
would agree that their path is for the few; the

Catholic Church combines Mantra Yoga with its Bhakti Yoga.

It is by means of formula that the occultist selects and concentrates the forces he wishes to work with. These formulae are based upon the Qabalistic Tree of Life, and whatever system he may be working, whether he be assuming the God-forms of Egypt or evoking the inspiration of Iacchus with chant and dance, he has the diagram of the Tree at the back of his mind. It is in the symbolism of the Tree that Western initiates are drilled, and it supplies the essential ground plan of classification to which all other systems can be related. The Ray upon which the Western aspirant works has manifested itself through many different cultures and developed a characteristic technique in each. The modern initiate works a synthetic system, sometimes using an Egyptian, a Greek, or even a Druidic method, for different methods are best suited for different purposes and conditions. In all cases, however, the operation he designs is strictly related to the Paths of the Tree of which he is master. If he possesses the grade which corresponds to the Sephirah Netzach, he can work with the manifestation of the force of that aspect of the Godhead (distinguished by the Qabalists by the name of Tetragrammaton Elohim) in

whatever system he may select. In the
Egyptian system it will be the Isis of Nature;
in the Greek, Aphrodite; in the Nordic, Freya;
in the Druidic, Keridwen. In other words, he
possesses the powers of the Sphere of Venus
in whatever traditional system he may be
using. Having attained a grade in one system,
he has access to the equivalent grades of all
the other systems of his Tradition.

But although he may use these other systems
as occasion serves, experience proves
that the Qabalah supplies the best
groundwork and the best system upon which
to train a student before he begins to
experiment with the pagan systems. the
Qabalah is essentially monotheistic; the
potencies it classifies are always regarded as
the messengers of God and not His fellow-
workers. This principle enforces the concept
of a centralized government of the Cosmos
and of the grip of the Divine Law upon the
whole of manifestation-a very necessary
principle with which to imbue any student of
the Arcane forces. It is the purity, sanity, and
clarity of the Qabalistic concepts as resumed
in the formula of the Tree of Life which
makes that glyph such an admirable one for
the meditations that exalt consciousness and
justify us in calling the Qabalah the Yoga of
the West.

Ultimately, we must realize that the idea of
two paths is, once again, and illusory duality.
In reality, there is only one path. That is truly
understood when you reach a particular level
of consciousness. That even though you may
have thought you were on the left or right
path, ultimately you ended up in the same
place, with the same knowledge – and now
recognize the ignorance in the original
perceived duality.

CHAPTER 12

A Qabalistic Look at Malkuth

Qabalistically, we live on the sphere of Malkuth. This is one of the spheres on the Tree of Sephiroth. The word Malkuth means the Kingdom and it is situated at the base of the Pillar of Equilibrium (the Middle Pillar). Some other titles given to Malkuth are the Gate, the Gate of Death, the Gate of the Garden of Eden, and the Gate of Justice.

The highest spiritual experience one can have in Malkuth is the knowledge and conversation with the Holy Guardian Angel. Its virtue is discrimination, and its vice is avarice and inertia.

The symbols, esoterically, that represent Malkuth are the altar of the double cube, the equal armed cross, the magical circle and the triangle of art.

Malkuth is said to be the Sphere of the Earth; but we must not make the mistake of thinking that the Qabalists meant by Malkuth only the terrestrial sphere. They also meant the Earth-soul-that is to say, the subtle, psychic aspect of matter; the underlying noumenon[46] of the physical plane which gives rise to all physical phenomena.

Likewise with the four elements. These are not earth, air, fire, and water as known to the physicists, but are the four conditions in which energy can exist. The esotericist distinguishes these from their mundane counterparts by referring to them as the Air of the Wise, or the Earth of the Wise, as the case may be. That is to say, the Element of Air or of Earth as it is known to the initiate.

The physicist recognizes the existence of matter in three states. Firstly, as solid, wherein the particles of which it is composed adhere firmly to each other; secondly, liquid, in which the particles move freely over each other; thirdly – gaseous, in which the particles all try to get as far away from each other as possible, or in other words, to these three modes of matter, correspond to the three elements of Earth, Water, and Air, and electrical phenomena corresponds to the element of Fire. Esoteric Science classifies all phenomena manifesting upon the physical plane under these four headings, as giving the best clue to the real understanding of their nature; and it

---

[46] A thing as it is in itself, as distinct from a thing as it is knowable by the senses.

recognizes that any given force can pass from one stage to another under certain conditions, just as water can exist in a state of ice and steam as well as its normal fluidity.

The esotericist sees in Malkuth the end-result of all operations; not until the Pairs of Opposites have achieved the settled equilibrium which gives the state of Earth, or coherence, can they be said to have completed any given cycle of experience. When this is achieved, they build a permanent vehicle of manifestation and stereotype its reactions; the machinery of expression thus evolved becomes self-regulating and will continue to function with the minimum of attention, just as the human heart opens and shuts its valves with perfect regularity in response to a stereotyped cycle of nervous impulses and the pressure of the blood.

The great point to remember in connection with Malkuth is that herein is achieved discrimination. It is in the inertia of Malkuth that its virtue lies. All the other Sephiroth are in varying degrees mobile; even the Central Pillar only achieving equilibrium in function, just as a tight-rope walker achieves it.

Like all the other Sephiroth, Malkuth can only be understood when considered in relation to its neighbors. But in this case, there is only one neighbor - Yesod[47]. No understanding of Malkuth can be arrived at save through an understanding of Yesod.

For while Malkuth is essentially the sphere of form, all coherence of parts, save simple mechanical stresses and electromagnetic attractions and repulsions, depend upon the functions of Yesod. And Yesod, though it is essentially a form-giving Sephirah, depends for the manifestation of its activities, upon the substance provided by the forms of Yesod and are such stuff as dreams are made of until they have picked up the material particles of Malkuth to body forth their forms. They are systems of stresses into whose framework the physical particles are built.

And equally with Malkuth, it is inanimate matter until the powers of Yesod ensoul it.

We should conceive of the material plane as the outward and visible sign of invisible, etheric activity. Malkuth, in its prime essence, is only known to the instruments of the physicist. It goes without saying that where there is life, there is Yesod, because Yesod is the vehicle of life; but it should also be realized that where there is any kind of

------

[47] "Foundation". Another sphere on the Tree of Sephiroth.

electrical activity or conductivity, whether of crystals, metals, or chemicals, there is Yesodic force in function. It is this fact which makes certain substances suitable for use as talismans, because they will take a charge of astral force.

It is not possible in these pages to go into a detailed study of esoteric physics; enough must be said, however, to give the student an understanding of the principles underlying this concept of the material world, which sees it as visible drapery upon an invisible framework.

The exact nature of the relationship between Yesod and Malkuth must be clearly understood because it is all-important for practical occult work. Yesod is, of course, the form-giving principle, and whatever form is built up in its Sphere will be bodied forth in the Sphere of Malkuth unless it contains incompatibles, for it will tend to draw to itself the conditions of material expression. Material particles, however, are extremely resistant and unresponsive in their nature, and it is only by working upon the most tenuous aspect of matter, to which initiates give the name of the Element of Fire, that Yesodic forces can produce any effects. Once a response can be obtained from this Elemental Fire, the other Elements can in their turn be influenced.

Elemental Fire, however, is a kind of over-state of matter with which only the most advanced physics has any acquaintance. It might best be called a state of relationship rather than a thing in itself. Elemental Air might be described as a capacity to achieve these relationships, and as such, is the vital principle of physical life; for it is only in so far as matter has a capacity for organization that organic substance is possible. Elemental Water, the Water of the Wise, is just plain protoplasm; and Elemental Earth is inorganic matter.

Now each of these types of organized force and reaction-capacity has its own very definite nature, from which it will depart no hair's-breadth for any force in the manifested cosmos. But as there are definite interrelations of influence and expression between these four elemental states, it is possible, by using their influence, one over the other, to achieve results which for want of understanding are called magical. It is, of course, the method of magic to manipulate these tenuous elemental forms; but it is also the method of life to do the same thing, and if magic is to be anything more than auto-suggestion, it must use the methods of life-that is to say, it must work through the intermediation of protoplasm, for protoplasm, in its curious web-like structure, carries the subtle magnetic force of the Fire of

the Wise, transmitted through elemental air.
In other words, the operator has to use his
own body as a self-starter; for it is the
magnetism of his own protoplasm that
supplies the basis of manifestation of any
force that is being brought through into the
Sphere of Malkuth. Carried to its logical
conclusion, this is the principle of generation,
whether of protozoa or spermatozoa.

The modern concept of matter approximates
very closely to that which has been held by
esoteric science from time immemorial. What
our senses perceive are the phenomena
attributable to activities of different types of
force, usually in organization and
combination. Only through an understanding
of the nature of these forces is the nature of
matter to be understood. Exoteric science is
dealing with the problem by refining its
concept of matter till there is no substance
left in it. What the physicist now knows as
matter is very far removed from the obvious.

The esotericist, approaching the problem
from the opposite direction, points out that
matter and mind are two sides of the same
coin, but that there comes a point in one's
investigation when it is profitable to change
over terminology, and talk of forces and
forms in terms of psychology, as if they were
conscious and purposive. This, he says,

234

enables us to deal with the phenomena we encounter much better than we can do if we limit ourselves to terms only applicable to inanimate matter and blind, undirected force.

We must always, by the nature of our intellect, use analogy as a help to understanding; if the analogies we use on this level of the investigation are the analogies of inanimate matter, we shall find them so inadequate as to be very limiting and misleading, and darkeners of counsel in general.

If, however, we use the terminologies of life and intelligence and purposive will, duly diluted to the requirements of the very rudimentary state of development of that which we have to deal, we shall find we have an analogy which is illuminating instead of limiting, and which will lead on to advancement in understanding.

It is for this reason that the esotericist personifies the subtler forces and calls them Intelligences. He then proceeds to deal with them as if they were intelligent, and he finds that there is a subtle side of his own nature and consciousness which responds to them, and to which, he fondly believes, they respond. At any rate, whether the response is mutual or not, his powers of dealing with them are, by this means, greatly extended beyond those which he possesses when he regards them as "a fortuitous concourse of uncorrelated incidents."

Malkuth is the nadir of evolution, but it should be looked upon, not as the ultimate depth of unspirituality, but as the marking-buoy in a yacht Any yacht that puts about on to the homeward course before it has rounded the marking-buoy is disqualified. And so it is with the soul. If we try to escape from the discipline of matter before we have mastered the lessons of matter, we are not advancing heavenwards, but suffering from arrested development. It is these spiritual defectives who flock from one to another of the innumerable wildcat uplift organizations that come to us from the Far East and the Far West. They find in cheap idealism an escape from the rigorous demands of life. But this is not a way of advancement, but a way of retreat. Sooner or later, they have to face the fence and clear it. Life brings them up to it again and again, and presently begins to use the whip and spur of psychological sickness; for those who will not face life, dissociate; and dissociation is the prime cause of most of the ills that mind is heir to.

If we study the lessons of history we shall get much light on moral and spiritual problems from an unexpected angle. We see that all civilization and inspiration arose in the East; a point to which those who are of Eastern race or follow an Eastern tradition point proudly, saying that the West must sit at the feet of the East if it is to learn the secrets of life.

Now it cannot be denied that there are many things, especially the more recondite aspects of psychology, concerning which the East knows a great deal more than the West, and which we should be wise to learn; but it also cannot be denied that, having originated in the East, the growing-point of evolution is now to be found in the West, and that for every advance in the art of living on this terrestrial planet, the East must look to the West unless it is content to go back to the spinning-wheel standard of life. But let it not be forgotten that with the primitive standard of life, goes also the primitive standard of death. A primitive culture can only support a sparse population. A great many people have got to die, mostly the old and the young. When we return to Nature, she deals with us after her own manner with her red tooth and claw. The unsoftened impact of Nature is not a pleasant thing. When human beings get too thick on the ground, she Wipes them out with disease and starvation. With the white man's civilization goes the white man's sanitation. By refraining from all action one may achieve release from the bondage of the body more quickly and effectually than one bargains for, if among the actions refrained from are those connected with communal cleanliness in a densely populated land.

The Greeks understood the principle of Malkuth better than did anybody else, and they were the founders of the European culture. They taught us to see beauty in perfect proportion and function, and nowhere else. The frieze of figures upon the Grecian urn turned the mind of Keats to the contemplation of ideal Truth and Beauty. There can be no higher ideal than this for the finite mind to contemplate, for in it the Law and the prophets are lifted far above the grim forbiddings of the Mosaic code into the inspiration of an ideal to be pursued.

It is in the Sphere of Malkuth that civilization has wrought for the last thousand years. It does not require any astrologer to tell us that the Great War marked the end of an epoch, and that we are now in the dawn of a new phase. According to Qabalistic doctrine, the Lightning Flash, having come down the Tree till it ends in Malkuth, is now replaced by the symbolism of the Serpent of Wisdom, whose coils loop upwards on the Paths till its head rests beside Kether. The Lightning Flash represents the unconscious descent of force, building the planes of manifestation, passing from active to passive and back again in order that equilibrium may be maintained. The Serpent coiling upon the Paths represents the dawn of objective consciousness and is the symbol of initiation; by the Path whereon the initiates have gone, ahead of their time, evolution is beginning to go, taking with it those who know to jump aboard.

We see the growing-point of evolution, then, beginning to rise out of Malkuth and reach out towards Yesod. This means that science, both pure and applied, is passing beyond the study of inanimate matter and is beginning to take account of the etheric and psychic side of things. This changing phase is visible all around us for those who can read the signs of the times. We see it in medicine, in international relationships in industrial organization. Last, and most reluctantly, we see it making itself felt in the sciences of physiology and psychology, which cling tenaciously to a materialistic explanation of all things, and especially the life-processes, even after physics, which avowedly deals with inanimate matter, has abandoned the materialistic position and talks in terms of mathematics.

The occult division of Malkuth into the Four Elements gives us a very valuable key. We should regard matter as we know it as Earth of Malkuth. The different types of physical activity, whether in molecules or masses, can be classified under the two headings of anabolism and katabolism, that is to say the building-up and the breaking down processes; these can be classified in esoteric terminology as the Water or Air of Malkuth, and whatever is said by esoteric philosophy or pagan mythology in relation to these elements will be applicable to these two metabolic processes and The Fire of Malkuth is that subtle electro-magnetic aspect of matter which is the link with the processes of consciousness and life, and to it all life-myths apply.

When this principle of classification is understood, the terminology of the alchemists becomes less recondite and absurd, for it is seen that the classification into Four Elements really refers to four modes of manifestation on the physical plane. This method of classification is of very great value, because it enables the relationship and correspondence between the physical plane and the life-processes behind it to be readily seen. It is especially important in the study of physiology and pathology, and in its practical application it is a most important key to therapeutics. The more advanced physicians are beginning to feel their way towards this position, and the classifications of Paracelsus are being quoted today by more than one leader of medical thought. The concept of diathesis or constitutional predisposition is receiving attention. Psychotherapy, again, is beginning to see that the old classification into the four temperaments affords a useful guide to treatment, and that it does not do to handle everyone in the same way; nor yet that similar results always spring from similar causes in the realms of mind, because temperament intervenes and falsifies the results. For instance, apathy in the phlegmatic type may simply mean boredom; whereas the same degree of apathy in the sanguine type may mean a complete breakdown of the whole personality. The analogies between material and mental things can be very misleading; whereas the analogies between mental and material things can be very enlightening.

The four elements correspond to the four temperaments as described by Hippocrates, the four Tarot suits, the twelve signs of the Zodiac, and the seven planets. If the implications of these statements are worked out, it will be seen that herein are contained some very important keys.

The Element of Earth corresponds to the Phlegmatic Temperament; the suit of Pentacles; the signs of Taurus, Virgo, and Capricorn; and the planets Venus and Luna.

The Element of Water corresponds to the Bilious Temperament; the Suit of Cups; the signs of Cancer, Scorpio, and Pisces; and the planet Mars.

The Element of Air corresponds to the Choleric Temperament; the suit of Swords; the signs of Libra, Gemini, and Aquarius; and the planets Saturn and Mercury.

The Element of Fire corresponds to the Sanguine Temperament; the suit of Wands; the signs of Aries, Sagittarius and Leo; and the planets Sol and Jupiter.

It will be seen, then, that if we classify mundane affairs and phenomena in terms of the Four Elements, we shall immediately see their relationship to astrology and the Tarot. Now classification is the stage that immediately follows observation in scientific method. A very great deal of scientific work simply consists in these two processes; in fact, for the rank and file of science these represent the total range of their activities. If science is limited to these two activities, as it would be, if we listened to our more pedestrian scientists, it would be no more than a compiling of lists of natural phenomena, as if the brokers were in on the universe. But the imaginative scientist, who alone is worthy of the name of research worker, uses classification not so much as a means of putting things away tidily, but to enable him to recognize relationships.

From the imaginative scientist who perceives to the philosophic scientist who interprets is but a step; and from the philosophical scientist who interprets in terms of causation to the esoteric scientist who interprets in terms of purpose, and so links science to ethics, is but another step. It is the tragedy of Esoteric Science that its exponents have nearly always been inadequately equipped upon the plane of Malkuth, and consequently unable to coordinate their results with those obtained by workers in other fields. As long as we rest content with this state of affairs we shall continue to have muddle-headed thinking and credulous assumptions as our inalienable lot. Esoteric Science needs to observe the rule of the yacht race, and make each magical operation round the marking-buoy of Malkuth before it is reckoned to have achieved completion.

Let us now interpret this simile from the point of view of technical occultism. Every magical operation is designed to bring power down the planes into the reach of the operator, who then applies it to whatever ends he may design. Many operators are content if they can obtain purely subjective results-that is to say, a sense of exaltation; others aim at the production of psychic phenomena. It should be recognized, however, that no operation is completed until the process has been expressed in terms of Malkuth, or, in other words, has issued forth in action on the physical plane. If this is not done, the force that has been generated is not properly "earthed", and it is this loose force left lying around that causes the trouble in magical experiments. It may not cause trouble in a single experiment, as few operators generate enough power to cause anything, let alone trouble; but in a series of experiments the effect may be cumulative, and result in the general psychic upheaval and run of bad luck and queer happenings so often reported by experimenters. It is these sort of things that give experimental magic a bad name, and lead to its being regarded as dangerous and compared to drug addiction. The true analogy, however, would be with the dangers of X-ray research in its early days. It is faulty technique that gives rise to trouble, as it always must when active potencies are being handled. Perfect your technique and you get rid of your troubles and have a very potent force available for use.

The only means of transition from Yesod to Malkuth is through the mediumship of living substances. Now there are various degrees of

244

livingness. The esotericist recognizes life wherever there is organized form, for he says that life alone is the organizer of form, though in what are popularly called inorganic substances, the proportion of life is very small, and in some cases in some forms of inorganic matter, however, there is a by no means negligible proportion of life, just as in plants there is a by no means negligible proportion of intelligence. It is only recent advances in experimental work, notably those of Sir Jagindranath Bose, that have demonstrated this fact, but it has long been known empirically to the practical occultist. He has always made use of crystalline and metallic substances as storage arteries of subtle forces. He has always regarded silk as an insulator. He has, in fact, availed himself of the properties of the same substances that the electrician employs today. The best talismans are considered to be disks of pure metal engraved with suitable devices and kept wrapped in silk of a color appropriate to the force with which the talisman is charged. A precious stone, which is of course a colored crystal, is a very important part of certain operations, because it is held to act as a focus for the force. It is also a very important part of certain types of wireless receivers. The influence of colors on mental states is now well recognized. No worker is allowed to work for a lengthy period in the red-light rooms of the manufacturers of photographic supplies, because it is recognized that such workers are liable to emotional disturbance and even temporary mental unbalance. All these things we are rediscovering by means of modern scientific method and its instruments, but they were well known to the ancients, and their practical applications were worked out to an extent that is not dreamed of today, save among the few who are popularly known as "cranky."

Plants also we find credited with a varying degree of "psychic activity." This is especially attributed to aromatic plants. The ancients had an elaborate system of attribution of plants to the different forms of subtle force. Some of these, of course, are fantastic, but there are certain broad principles which give guidance. Wherever we find a plant traditionally associated with any deity we may be fairly certain that that plant has been proven to have affinities with the type of force that that deity represents. It may be that the association appears to our modern eyes to be superficial and irrational, such associations as Freud has shown us, that the dreaming mind employs; but the worshippers of the deity, if the association is hallowed by tradition, will have built up the psychic connection between the plant and the force, and as in all such traditional associations, once established, the link is easily recoverable by those who know how to make use of the constructive imagination. Whether there is any intrinsic relationship between the nature of the plant and the nature of the force to which it is assigned, as in the case of the rose to Venus and the lily to the Virgin Mary, such a relationship is speedily established by the worshippers of a cult, and, equally speedily recoverable by those who follow in their footsteps, even after a lapse of centuries. Therefore, for all practical purposes there is such a relationship, not only in relation to the plants assigned to a particular deity, but in relation to animals as well.

An attribution which has special practical importance is that of perfumes. Concerning the perfumes, it is less easy to lay down hard and fast rules, as the available perfumes are almost countless, and the forces in practical working often tend to run one into the other. For instance, it is difficult, and in fact undesirable, to keep the forces of Netzach separated from those of Tiphareth, or those of Hod from Yesod, or Yesod from Malkuth; and anyone who tries working Geburah without Gedulah would burn his fingers.

Perfumes are used not only to enable the deity to manifest, but to tune the imagination of the operator. To this latter end they are most efficacious, as anyone will discover for themselves if they try to work a ceremony without the appropriate perfume. With inexperienced operators it is advisable to dispense with the use of perfumes in case the psychic effect is too drastic for comfort or convenience.

Broadly speaking, we can divide perfumes into those which exalt consciousness and those which stir the subconscious to activity. Of those which exalt consciousness, the aromatic gums stand by themselves, and these are employed exclusively in the manufacture of ecclesiastical incense, in addition to these, certain essential oils possess similar properties, especially those which are aromatic and astringent rather than sweet and spicy. These substances are of value in all operations in which the aim is increased intellectual clarity or exaltation of the mystical type.

The perfumes that awaken the subconscious mind are of two types, the Dionysiac and the Venusian. The Dionysiac odors are of the aromatic, spicy type, such as smoldering cedar - or sandalwood or pinecones. The Venusian odors are of a sweet, cloying nature, such as in actual practice these two types of odors shade one into the other, and characteristic flower odors are to be found in both divisions. In the practical work of compounding the perfumes a blend of ingredients is almost always employed, as they enhance each other. Many perfumes which by themselves are crude and acrid, or cloying and sickly, become admirable when blended.

It has been said that synthetic perfumes are useless for magical work. In my experience this is not the case, provided the essence is of good quality. Good synthetic essences are indistinguishable from the natural products save by chemical tests. As the value of perfumes is psychological, their action being upon the operator, not upon the power invoked, the chemical nature of the substance is immaterial provided one gets the appropriate effect.

The same applies to precious stones, rank heresy though it be to say so. All one needs is a crystal of the appropriate color, and whether it is a Burmese ruby or a Burma one makes no difference to anything except one's bank balance. That the ancients knew this is witnessed by the fact that in the lists of precious stones sacred to various deities, alternative gems are always given. For instance, Crowley, in "777" gives pearls, moon-stones, crystal, and quartz as all being sacred to the moon-forces, and the ruby or any red stone as sacred to Mars.

It is believed by the occultist that the mental concentration of a current of will, backed by the imagination, has an effect upon certain crystals, metals, and oils. He makes a use of this property in order to conserve in them forces of a particular type so that these forces can be readily re-awakened at will, or even exercise their influence all the time by means of a steady emanation. Most ceremonial depends in some degree at least upon the principle of the consecrated magical weapons. It is noteworthy that all the more important equipment of a church is always consecrated before it is taken into use. Whether this consecration is effective is not a matter of opinion. Any good psychic will readily distinguish between consecrated and unconsecrated objects, provided, of course, that the consecration has been effectual. It is a matter of experience with any practical occultist that a very definite change takes place in him when he takes his accustomed magical instruments in hand or puts on his accustomed robes. He can do with these what he cannot do without them. He also knows that it takes time to "break in" a new magical instrument. It is interesting to note in this respect that I am quite unable to write anything about the mystical side of the Qabalah without my ancient and battered "Tree of Life" beside me. It is also interesting to note that when this Tree of Life, which was originally prepared for me by someone else, became so dingy as to be almost undecipherable, I repainted it myself, and found thereafter that it immediately took on a marked increase in magnetism: thus bearing out the old tradition that one should always prepare one's magical weapons as far as possible with one's own hands.

The great problem in the practical working is to bring things through to the Sphere of Malkuth. Many methods are described by the ancients – with how much truth one has no means of knowing. How far were actual materializations obtained by the method of blood-sacrifice described by Virgil, and how far did the exalted imagination of the participants in these awe-inspiring rites supply the basis of manifestation?

But whatever may be the facts, the holocausts of the ancients are not a practicable method for the modern experimenter to follow. The basis of the idea, however, lies in the fact that freshly shed blood gives off ectoplasm. There are, of course, materializing mediums who also give off ectoplasm without the shedding of blood. But those who give off an appreciable quantity are few and far between. When a number of psychically developed people are gathered together in a circle for the purpose of evocation they may, between them, give off sufficient ectoplasm to form the necessary basis for physical phenomena. Such a method is not without its difficulties, not to say risks, and the esotericist, who is a philosopher rather than an experimenter, seldom makes use of it. It is sufficient for him if he gets manifestations in the Sphere of Yesod and perceives them with the inner vision.

The only satisfactory channel of evocation is the operator himself. In the Egyptian method of evocation, known as the assumption of the god-forms, the operator identifies himself with the god and offers himself as the channel of manifestation. It is his own magnetism that bridges the gulf between Malkuth and Yesod. There is no other method so satisfactory, for the amount of magnetism in a living being is far greater than in any metal or crystal, however precious.

This ancient method is also known to us under another name; it is called by moderns, mediumship. When the spirit speaks through the entranced medium, precisely the same thing is happening as happened in ancient Egypt when the priest with the mask of Horus spake with the voice of Horus.

When we consider the microcosmic Tree, the physical body is Malkuth; the etheric double is

Yesod; the astro-mental body is Hod and Netzach; and the higher mind is Tiphareth. Whatever the higher mind can conceive can readily be brought through into manifestation in the subjective Malkuth. We do better to rely upon this method of evocation rather than the extraneous devices of extruded ectoplasm or the outpouring of vital fluids, even if this latter device were practicable in our modern civilization.

The best magical weapon is the magus himself, and all other contrivances are but a means to an end, the end being that exaltation and concentration of consciousness which makes a magus of an ordinary man. "Know ye not that ye are the temple of the living God?" said a Great One. If we know how to use the symbolic furniture of this living temple, we have the keys of heaven in our hands.

The key to this use is given in the microcosmic attributions of the Tree. Interpreting these in terms of function, and function in terms of spiritual principles, we can unlock the door of the Storehouse of Force. The best and most complete manifestation of the power of God is through the energized enthusiasm of the trained and dedicated man. We would be wiser if we looked for the end-result of a magical operation to come about through natural channels rather than to expect an interference with the course of Nature-an expectation that in the very nature of things is doomed to disappointment.

Let us make this clear by illustration. Supposing we desire to heal sickness, we should, working by the method of the Tree, employ a rite or meditation of Tiphareth. But are we, for this reason, to limit our operations to the Sphere of Tiphareth and require the healing to be a purely Spiritual healing, as do the Christian Scientists? Or shall we modify our method sufficiently to allow of the laying on of glands and the anointing with oil, which are operations of the Sphere of Yesod, designed to conduct magnetic force? Or shall we, which appears to me the wiser method, make use of an operation of Malkuth also, thus bringing the power steadily down the planes into manifestation without break or gap in the transmutation and conduction?

And what is an operation of the Sphere of Malkuth? It is simply action on the physical plane. In an invocation of healing, therefore, I think we do better to invoke the Great Physician to manifest His power to us through the human physician, for that is the natural channel, than to rely upon a spiritual force for which the only channel of evocation

is the spiritual nature of the patient, who may
or may not be able to rise to the occasion.

That great spiritual forces can be brought to
bear effectually upon the healing of our
diseases is beyond question, but they must
have a channel of manifestation; and why be
at great pains to build a psychic one when
there is a natural one ready to hand? God
moves in a mysterious way. His wonders to
perform when natural law is a sealed book to
us; but when we understand the ways of
Nature's working, we see that God moves in a
perfectly natural way, through the regularly
established channels; the difference between
the supernatural and the natural does not lie
in the channels of manifestation that are used,
but in the amount of power that comes
through them. Not in quality but in quantity
does the flow of power alter when spiritual
forces are successfully invoked.

The whole problem of Malkuth is a problem
of channels and connecting the rest of the
work is done by the mind on the subtler
planes; the real difficulty lies in the transition
from the subtle to the dense, for the subtle is
so ill-equipped to work on the dense. This
transition is affected by means of the
magnetism of living things, whether organic
or inorganic.

Three ideas issue from a contemplation of the Yetziratic Text related to Malkuth - the concept of the Resplendent Intelligence which illuminates the splendor of all the Lights; the relationship between Malkuth and Binah; and the function of Malkuth in causing an influence to emanate from the Angel of Kether.

It may seem a curious idea that Malkuth, which is the material world, should be the illuminator of the Lights; we can understand this, however, if we refer to the analogy of physics, which tells us that the sky only appears blue and luminous owing to the reflection of light from the innumerable dust particles floating in the atmosphere; absolutely dustless air is unilluminated, and our sky would have the darkness of interstellar space if it were not for these dust particles. We also learn from the study of physics that we see objects solely by means of the rays of light they reflect from their surfaces. When there is little or no reflection, as with black cloth, it is almost invisible in a dim light, a property made much use of by conjurers and illusionists.

It is the formative, concreting function of Malkuth which finally renders tangible and definite what was, upon the higher planes, intangible and indefinite, and this is its great

256

service to manifestation and its characteristic power. All the Lights, that is to say the emanations of all the other Sephiroth, become illuminated, visible, when reflected from the concrete aspects of Malkuth.

Every magical operation must come through to Malkuth before it can be reckoned to have attained completion, for only in Malkuth is the force finally locked home into form. Therefore all magical work is better carried out in the form of a ritual performed on the physical plane, even if the operator is working alone, than simply as a form of meditation operating upon the astral plane only. There must be something upon the physical plane, even if it be no more than lines drawn on a talisman, or the writing of signs upon the air, which brings the action through to the plane of Malkuth. Experience proves that an operation so terminated is a very different matter to an operation which begins and ends on the astral.

The relationship between Malkuth and Binah is very clearly indicated in the titles assigned to both these Sephiroth. Binah is the Superior Mother and Malkuth the Inferior Mother. As we have already seen, Binah is the primordial Giver of Form. Malkuth being the Sphere of Form, the relationship is obvious. That which had its inception in Binah has its culmination in Malkuth. This point gives us an important clue by means of which to guide our research among the ramifications of the polytheistic pantheons. The Qabalistic system is explicit concerning the doctrine of Emanations, whereby the One unfolds into the Many, and the Many are reabsorbed into the One. No other system is specific upon this point, though in all of them it is hinted under the guise of genealogies. The begettings and matings of the gods and goddesses, by no means always in holy wedlock, give definite indication of the implicit doctrines of emanation and polarity, and are not merely ribald phantasies of primitive man, creating the gods in his own image and likeness.

A careful comparison of the information that has come down to us concerning the rites by which the ancients worshipped their many gods soon reveals that the clear-cut myths so delightfully retold for children have little bearing on the actual religion of the folk who used them as the means of expression for spiritual teachings. The gods and goddesses melt one into the other in the most perplexing fashion, so that we get the Bearded Venus, and Hercules, of all persons, arrayed in female clothes.

It is clear from a study of ancient art that the persons and characteristics of the various

gods and goddesses were used as a form of
picture-writing to indicate definite abstract
ideas, of which the convention was well
understood by the priesthood. Having to deal
with an illiterate population for the most part,
for learning was limited to a very few in those
days, they wisely said, 'look on this symbol
and think about this story; you may not know
what it means, if you are looking in the right
direction, the direction whence light arises;
and in proportion as you are able to receive it,
light will flow into your soul if you
contemplate these ideas'. It is probable to the
point of certainty that the illumination given
in the Mysteries included the elucidation of
the metaphysics of these myths.

Persephone, Diana, Aphrodite, Hera, all
exchange their symbols, functions,
characteristics, and even subordinate titles in a
bewildering manner in Greek myths and art.
Likewise do Priapos, Pan, Apollo, and Zeus.
The best we can say of them is that all the
goddesses are Great Mothers, and all the gods
are Givers of Life; the difference between
them lying not in function but in the level
upon which they function. A distinction is
drawn between the Celestial Venus and the
goddess of earthly love of the same name; the
discerning can see an equal distinction, and an
equal underlying identity, between Zeus the
All-Father, and Priapos, equally addicted to

fatherhood, but after another manner, the one being earthly where the other is celestial. Nevertheless, they are not two gods, but one god: just as Binah and Malkuth are not two distinct types of force, but the same force functioning on different levels. This is the key to the understanding of the significance of phallic worship, which plays so important a part in all ancient and primitive faiths, a part so little understood by their scholastic interpreters. Its real meaning is the bringing down of the godhead into manhood in the hope of taking manhood up into godhead. A process which is also the basis of the Freudian therapy.

The statement that Malkuth causes an influence to emanate from the Angel of Kether further bears out this idea. We see that the Great Mother, which is Malkuth, polarizes with the All-Father, which is Kether.

This classification, however, is too simple to serve us adequately, whether we are reducing a pagan pantheon to its simplest terms or dealing with the chances and changes of personal life. But in the four quarters, or elements, into which Malkuth is divided, we find the key that we need.

These four elements are said to be the Earth, Air, Fire, and Water of the Wise-that is to say, four types of activity. They are represented in the notation of esoteric science by four different types of triangles. Fire is represented by a triangle point upwards; Air by a similar triangle with a bar across it, thus indicating that Air may be esteemed as akin in nature to Fire, but denser. In fact, we should not go far wrong if we called Air, Negative Fire, or Fire. Positive Water is represented by a triangle point downwards, and Earth by the same triangle with a bar across it; and to these two symbols the same principles apply as to their predecessors.

Supposing, then, we consider the Fire triangle as representing unconditioned force and the Air triangle as representing conditioned force, the Earth triangle as representing totally inert form and the Water triangle as representing an active type of form, we have another mode of classification in the most ancient myths, the air, or space-god, is the parent of the sun, celestial fire, and water is the matrix of earth. This comes out clearly on the Central Pillar of the Tree of Life, where Kether, space, overshadows Tiphareth, the sun-center, and the watery Yesod, the moon-center, overshadows the earthy Malkuth.

Or supposing we arrange the symbols composing the glyph after another manner, which it is the glory of the Tree that it enables

us to do, and place them as the four
Elements, citrine, olive, russet, and black, in
the sphere of Malkuth, and consider the life-
force descending from Kether as operating
after the manner of an alternating current of
electricity, which the doctrine of alternating
polarity teaches us to do, we find that force
will sometimes be flowing from Malkuth to
Kether, and sometimes from Kether to
Malkuth.

Now this is an all-important point when
applied to the microcosm, for it teaches us
that we need to be in circuit with the Earth-
soul just as much as with the God of Heaven;
there is an inspiration that rises up from the
unconscious quite as much as there is an
inspiration that flows down from the
superconscious.

This comes out clearly in the Greek myths,
wherein we find such positive earth forces as
Pan, who, by virtue of his goat-symbolism,
cannot be assigned otherwise than to the
Sphere of Earth, for Capricorn is the earthiest
of the earthy triplicity. Pan represents the
positive magnetism of the earth up rushing in
its return to the All-Father. Ceres, on the
other hand, or many-breasted Diana, who are
both very earthly Venuses and far from virgin,
represent the final earthing of the heavenly
force in dense matter. Hera, who has been

called the Celestial Venus or heavenly
Aphrodite, represents the return of the up-
rushing earth-force to heaven, and is earth-
positive on a celestial level.

These are things difficult to elucidate to those
who have not seen the sun at midnight. They
yield much to meditation, but little to
disputation.

In the Sphere of Malkuth are worked all
divinations. Now the object of any method of
divination is to find a set of things on the
physical plane which correspond accurately
and comprehensively to the invisible forces in
the same way that the movements of the
hands of a clock correspond to the passage of
time.

For revealing general trends and conditions it
is agreed by universal experience of those who
have studied such matters that astrology is the
best system of correspondences. But for
obtaining an answer to a single question it is
not sufficiently specific, for too many factors
may come in to modify the result. The
initiated diviner, therefore, makes use of the
more specific systems, such as divination by
the Tarot or geomancy, when he wants to
obtain an answer to a specific question.

263

But it is of little use to go into a shop and buy a pack of Tarot cards unless there is the knowledge necessary to build up the astral correspondences to each card. This takes time, as there are seventy-two cards to work with. Once it is done, however, the operator can take the cards into his hands with a considerable degree of confidence that his subconscious mind, whatever that may be, will all unwittingly deal the cards that refer to the matter in question. Exactly how the shuffle and deal is affected we do not know, but one thing is certain, when the Great Angel of the Tarot has been contacted, the cards are remarkably revealing.

Having considered the general principles of the Sphere of Malkuth, we are now in a position to study its special symbolism with profit.

It is called the Kingdom, in other words, the sphere ruled by the King-and the King is the title of Microprosopos, who consists of the six central Sephiroth, excluding the Three Supernals. We may regard Malkuth, or the material Sphere, as the sphere of manifestation of these six central Sephiroth, which themselves are emanated by the Three Supernals. Everything then, ends in Malkuth, even as everything begins in Kether.

The Magical Image of Malkuth is a young woman, crowned and veiled; this is the Isis of Nature, her face veiled to show that the spiritual forces are hidden within the outer form. This idea is also present in the symbolism of Binah, which is summed up in the concept of "the outer robe of concealment." Malkuth, as is clearly set forth in the Yetziratic Text, is Binah upon a lower arc.

Now Binah is called the Dark Sterile Mother, and Malkuth is called the Bride of Microprosopos, or the Bright Fertile Mother, and these correspond to the dual aspects of the Egyptian moon-goddess as Isis and Hathor, Isis being the positive aspect of the goddess, and Hathor the negative aspect. In Greek symbolism these would correspond to Aphrodite and Ceres. Now, Aphrodite is the positive aspect of the female potency, for be it remembered that under the law of alternating polarity, that which is negative on the outer planes is positive on the inner, and vice versa. Aphrodite, the Celestial Venus, is the giver of magnetic stimulus to the spiritually negative male; it is because her function is not understood in modern life that so much is wrong with modern life. Binah, the higher aspect of Isis, is, however, barren, because the positive pole is always the giver of the stimulus, but never the producer of the result.

265

The Malkuth aspect of Isis is the Bright
Fertile Mother, the goddess of fecundity, thus
indicating the end-result of the operation of
Isis on the physical plane.

The situation of Malkuth at the foot of the
Pillar of Equilibrium places it in the direct line
of the descent of power from Kether,
transmuted in Daath, the Invisible Sephirah,
and passing on to the planes of form via
Tiphareth. This is the Path of Consciousness,
whereas the two Side Pillars are Paths of
Function; but the two Side Pillars also
converge on Malkuth via the Thirty-first and
Twenty-ninth Paths. Consequently, everything
ends in Malkuth.

We who are incarnated in physical bodies are
standing in Malkuth, and when we set out
upon the Way of Initiation our route lies up
the Thirty-second Path to Yesod. This Path,
straight up the Central Pillar, is called the Path
of the Arrow, which is shot from Qesheth,
the Bow of Promise; it is by this route that the
mystic rises upon the planes; the initiate,
however, adds to his experience the powers of
the Side Pillars as well as the realizations of
the Middle Pillar.

This aspect of the Central Pillar is expressed
in the Yetziratic Text wherein it states that
Malkuth causes an influence to emanate from

the Prince of Countenances, the Angel of Kether.

The additional titles assigned to Malkuth bring out its attributes clearly. It is regarded as the Gate and the Mate. These two ideas are in essence one idea, for the womb of the Mother is the Gate of Life. It is also the Gate of Death, for birth into the plane of form is death to higher things.

Malkuth is also said to be Kallah, the Bride of Microprosopos, and Malkah, the Queen of Malekh, the King. This clearly indicates the function in polarity that prevails between the planes of form and the planes of force; the planes of form being the female aspect, polarized and made fertile by the influences of the planes of force.

The God-name in Malkuth is Adonai Malekh, or Adonai ha Aretz, which titles mean, the Lord who is King, and the Lord of Earth. Herein we clearly see the assertion of the supremacy of the One God in the Kingdoms of Earth, and every magical operation, wherein the operator takes power into his own hands, should commence with the invocation of Adonai to indwell his temple of earth and rule therein, that no force may break from its allegiance to the One.

Those who call upon the Name of Adonai call upon God made manifest in Nature, which is the aspect of God adored by initiates of the Nature Mysteries, whether Dionysian or Isiac-which concern the different ways of opening super-consciousness via subconsciousness.

The archangel is the great angel Sandalphon, who is sometimes called by Qabalists the Dark Angel; whereas Metatron, the Angel of the Countenance, is the Bright Angel. These two angels are held to stand behind the right and left shoulders of the soul in its hours of crisis. They might be taken to represent good and bad karma. It is in reference to the function of Sandalphon as the Dark Angel presiding over the Karmic Debt that Malkuth is called the Gate of Justice and the Gate of Tears. It has been said by a wit, with more truth than he knew, that this planet was actually some other planet's hell. It is in very fact the sphere in which karma is normally worked out. Where there is sufficient knowledge, however, karma can be worked out deliberately on the subtler planes, and this method is one of the forms of spiritual healing.

The Order of Angels assigned to Malkuth are the Ashim, the Souls of Fire, or Fiery Particles, of which Madam Blavatsky says some very interesting things. A Soul of Fire is in actual fact the consciousness of an atom; the Ashim therefore represent the natural consciousness of dense matter; it is these which bestow on it its characteristics. It is these Fiery Lives, these infinitesimal electrical charges, which are forever weaving backwards and forwards with tremendous activity in the background of matter and form its basis. Everything that we know as matter builds up on this groundwork. It is with the help of these Fiery Lives that certain types of magic are worked. There are but few who can work such magic, for the denser the plane to be manipulated, the greater must be the power of the Magus who commands it.

The Mundane Chakra of Malkuth is the Sphere of the Elements. These we have already considered in such detail as is possible in these pages.

The Spiritual Experience of Malkuth is the Vision of the Holy Guardian Angel. Now this angel, which according to the Qabalists is assigned to each soul at birth and companions him till death, when it takes him into its keeping and presents him before the face of God for judgment, is in actuality the Higher Self of each one of us, which builds up around the Divine Spark that is the nucleus of the soul and endures for an evolution, sending down a process into matter at each incarnation to form the basis of the new personality.

When the Higher Self and the Lower Self become united through the complete absorption of the lower by the higher, true adepthood is gained; this is the Great Initiation, the Lesser Divine Union. It is the supreme experience of the incarnate soul, and when this takes place, it is freed from any compulsion to rebirth into the prison-house of flesh. Thenceforth it is free to go on up the planes and enter into its rest, or, if it so elects, to remain within the earth-sphere and function as a Master.

This, then, is the spiritual experience which is assigned to Malkuth-the bringing down of the Godhead into manhood, just as the spiritual experience of Tiphareth is the taking up of manhood into the Godhead.

The especial virtue of Malkuth is said to be Discrimination. This idea is further carried out in the curious symbolism of the ancients which declared the correspondence in the microcosm to be with the anus. Whatever in life is effete has to be excreted, and the macrocosmic excretion is into the Qliphothic spheres which depend below Malkuth, whence the cosmic excreta cannot return to the planes of organized form until they find balance in equilibrium. There is, therefore, in the Qliphothic world, a sphere which is not Hell, but Purgatory; it is a reservoir of disorganized force emanated from broken-up forms, cast out from evolution; it is Chaos upon a lower arc. It is from this reservoir of force that is accustomed to form, and therefore organizes readily, that the Shells, or imperfect entities, build up their vehicles. It is also said to be drawn upon for the lower types of magic of an evil kind. The tendency of such forces as are available in the Qliphothic sphere must always be to assume once more such forms as they were accustomed to before they were disintegrated and reduced to their primal state; as these forms were at least out of date, if not actively evil, it naturally follows that this matter of chaos is not a desirable substance to work in; and had best be left there till its purification is complete and it has filtered back through the Sphere of Earth by the natural channels, and been drawn once again into the stream of evolution. It is for this reason that all the underworld cults and the evocation of the departed are undesirable, for the forms the manifesting entities assume must be built in part at least of this substance of Chaos.

It is the especial virtue of Malkuth, then, to act as a kind of cosmic filter, casting out the effete and preserving that which still retains its usefulness.

The characteristic vices of the functioning of Malkuth are said to be avarice and inertia. It is easy to see how the stability of Malkuth can be overdone, and so give rise to sluggishness and inertia. The concept of avarice, though not so obvious upon the surface, soon yields its significance to investigation; for the over-retentiveness of avarice is a kind of spiritual costiveness, the exact opposite of the discrimination which rejects the excreta of life through the cosmic anus into the cosmic cesspool of the Qliphoth. It is interesting to note that Freud declares that the miser is invariably constipated, and associates the dream of money with feces.

One of the most important things we have to do before we can rise out of the limitations of life in Malkuth and breathe a wider air, is to learn how to let go; how to sacrifice the lesser to the greater and so buy the pearl of great price. It is discrimination which enables us to know which is the lesser value that has to be given up in order to obtain the greater, for there is no gain without sacrifice. What we do not realize is that every sacrifice should yield a substantial profit in treasure laid up in heaven where neither moth nor rust do corrupt; otherwise, it is mere useless waste.

We have already noted one of the
correspondences assigned to Malkuth in the
microcosm. It is also said, however, that
Malkuth corresponds to the feet of the Divine
Man. Here again we have an important
concept; for unless the feet are firmly planted
on Mother Earth, no stability is possible.
There are altogether too many top-heavy
mystics who like to think that the Divine Man
ends at the neck like a cherub, and give no
place to the generative organs of Yesod, or
the anus of Malkuth. They need to learn the
lesson that the heavenly dream taught to St
Peter, that nothing which God made is
unclean unless we allow it to become so. We
should recognize the Divine Life in all its
functions, and so bring the manhood up into
Godhead and sanctify it. Cleanliness is next to
godliness, especially internal cleanliness. If we
evade and avoid a thing, how are we to keep it
clean and wholesome? The taboos of a
primitive people have been altogether
overdone in our civilized life, with disastrous
consequences to the health and
wholesomeness of humanity.

The symbols of Malkuth are the altar of the
double cube and the equal-armed cross, or
cross of the elements.

The altar of the double cube is symbolic of
the Hermetic maxim, "As above, so below,"

273

and teaches that what is visible is the
reflection of what is invisible, and
corresponds with it exactly. This cubical altar
is the altar of the Mysteries, in
contradistinction to the table-altar, which is
the altar of the Church. For the table-altar
stands in the east, but the cubical altar stands
in the center. It is said to be in proper
proportion when it is the height of the navel
of a six-foot man, and its breadth and depth
are half its height.

The equal-armed cross, or cross of the
elements, represents the four elements in
balanced equilibrium, which is the perfection
of Malkuth. It is represented on the Tree by
the division of Malkuth into four quarters,
colored citrine, olive, russet, and black, with
the citrine towards Yesod and the black
towards the Qliphoth; the olive towards
Netzach and the russet towards Hod. These
are the reflections of the Three Pillars and the
Qliphothic sphere, dulled and tempered by
the veil of earth.

Thus are all things summed up in Malkuth,
though seen in a glass darkly, by reflection,
and not face to face.

The four Tarot cards yield curious results
when subjected to meditation in the light of
what we know about Malkuth. The Ten of

Wands is called the Lord of Oppression; the Ten of Cups, the Lord of Perfected Success; the Ten of Swords, the Lord of Ruin; and the Ten of Pentacles, the Lord of Wealth.

As we have already seen, it is in Malkuth that spiritual forces come to their fulfilment on the plane of form, and by taking these completed forms, and "sacrificing" them, we can translate them back into spiritual potencies. These four Tarot cards, it will be observed, are alternately good and bad in their significance; in fact, the Ten of Swords is said to be the worst card in the pack to divination. There is a curious alchemical doctrine which has a bearing on this point. It is taught that the signs of the planets are compounded out of three symbols – the solar disk, the lunar crescent, and the cross of corrosion or sacrifice; and these symbols, rightly interpreted, give the key to the alchemical nature of the planet and its practical use in the Great Work of transmutation. For instance, Mars, in whose symbol the cross surmounts the circle, is said to be outwardly corrosive, but inwardly solar; Venus, in which the circle surmounts the cross, is said to be outwardly solar, but inwardly corrosive, or in the words of Scripture, sweet in the mouth, but in the belly bitter.

In these four Tarot tens the same principle is seen to prevail. Each card represents the working of a certain type of spiritual force on the plane of dense matter. The most spiritual of these cards, the ten of the suit whose ace is said to be the Root of the Powers of Fire, is called the Lord of Oppression. This reaches us that the higher spiritual forces are apt to be outwardly corrosive when operating upon the plane of matter. The powers of Fire, at their highest potency in the ten of Wands, are a refining fire. "As gold is tried in the furnace, so the heart must be tried by pain."

On the other hand, all the symbolism of the suit of Cups, or Chalices, shows the Venusian influence very clearly; it is in this suit we find the Lords of Pleasure, Material Happiness, and Abundance. But we also find the Lords of Illusory Success, Abandoned Success, and Loss in Pleasure, which shows clearly that this suit, though outwardly solar, is inwardly corrosive.

Swords, again, are under the Martian influence, and the Lord of Ruin shows the total sacrifice of all material things.

But in Pentacles, earth of earth, the position is again reversed, and we find that the ten of Pentacles is the Lord of Wealth.

It will be seen, therefore, that those cards which are of suits primarily spiritual in nature are outwardly corrosive on the physical plane; and those cards of suits that are primarily material in nature are outwardly solar, or beneficent on the material plane. This teaches a very useful lesson, and gives a very important key when used in those systems of divination which are designed to give discernment of the spiritual influences operating in a case.

All mundane affairs rise and fall like the waves of the sea, crest following trough, and trough following crest in rhythmical progression; therefore, when any mundane condition is at either its zenith or nadir, we know that a change of tide is to be expected in the near future. This knowledge is embodied in many popular sayings, such as "It's a long lane that has no turning," and "The darkest hour is before the dawn." Harriman, the great American millionaire, said that he made his fortune by always buying on a falling market and selling on a rising one-which is the exact opposite to what everyone else tries to do. Nevertheless, it is a farsighted proceeding, for a boom always topples over into a depression, and a depression issues forth into a boom. This has happened so often even within living memory that one would have thought speculators would have learnt the lessons of history, but they never do. It was a knowledge of this fact that enabled the Fraternity of the Inner Light to be piloted steadily amidst the post-war difficulties, and come through without having to curtail any of its activities. There are times when it is necessary to be modest in order to be solvent; but there are times when one can launch out boldly, despite all outward seeming, because one knows that the tide is rising under one.

These four cards, then, give a very true insight into the nature of the operation of forces in Malkuth, and when they turn up in a divination, one always prepares for the outward gold to turn to corrosion, and the outward corrosion to turn to gold sooner or later, and one takes in or spreads one's sails accordingly.

This is the true use of divination-to enable one to discern the spiritual forces concerned in any happening, and act accordingly. Of what use, then, is the divination performed by one who has not spiritual discernment? And can one expect to find spiritual discernment in the hack occultist who gives so much for half-a-crown, and so much more for ten shillings? Spiritual things are not done in this way. Among the ancients, divination was a religious rite, and so it should be among us, if it is not to bring a trail of bad luck in its wake.

CHAPTER 13

The Correct Understanding of Magic and its Role in Evolution

The word magic has been greatly misunderstood in the current age. It has been reduced to mere fantasy and not viewed as it should be, as something of the highest value and the divine wisdom of the Gods. Again, this is due to the mass mind's degradation further into Eikasia. The mass mind is now not able to distinguish between actual fantasy and what it thinks is fantasy because the imagination is running wild. The mass mind would rather imagine extra-terrestrials and other ridiculous things than see what the highly evolved and intelligent ancient people left us a guide.

There is a school of Philosophy still in existence of which modern culture has lost sight. Glimpses of it are discernible in the ancient philosophies with which all educated men are familiar, but these are hardly more intelligible than fragments of forgotten sculpture, — less so, for we comprehend the human form, and can give imaginary limbs to a torso, but we can give no imaginary meaning to the hints coming down to us from Plato or

Pythagoras, pointing, for those who hold the clue to their significance, to the secret knowledge of the ancient world. Side lights, nevertheless, may enable us to decipher such language, and a very rich intellectual reward offers itself to persons who are willing to attempt the investigation. For, strange as the statement will appear at first sight, modern metaphysics, and to a large extent modern physical science, have been groping for centuries blindly after knowledge which occult philosophy has enjoyed in full measure all the while.

Owing to a train of fortunate circumstances, we have come to know that this is the case, we have come into some contact with persons who are heirs of a greater knowledge concerning the mysteries of Nature and humanity than modern culture has yet evolved, and our present wish is to sketch the outlines of this knowledge, to record with exactitude the experimental proofs we have obtained that occult science invests. Its adepts with a control of natural forces superior to that enjoyed by physicists of the ordinary type, and the grounds there are for bestowing the most respectful consideration on the theories entertained by occult science concerning the constitution and destinies of the human soul. Of course people in the present day will be slow to believe that any knowledge worth considering can be found outside the bright focus of European culture. Modern science has accomplished grand results by the open method of investigation, and is very impatient of the theory that persons who ever attained to real knowledge, either in sciences or metaphysics, could have been content to hide their light under a bushel.

So, the tendency has been to conceive that occult philosophers of old — Egyptian priests, Chaldean Magi, Essenes, Gnostics, theurgic Neo-Platonists, and the rest — who kept their knowledge secret, must have adopted that policy to conceal the fact that they knew very little. Mystery can only have been loved by charlatans who wished to mystify. The conclusion is pardonable from the modern point of view, but it has given rise to an impression in the popular mind that the ancient mystics have actually been turned inside out and found to know very little. This impression is absolutely erroneous. Men of science in former ages worked in secret, and instead of publishing their discoveries, taught them in secret to carefully selected pupils. Their motives for adopting that policy are readily intelligible, even if the merits of the policy may seem still open to discussion. At all events, their teaching has not been forgotten, it has been transmitted by secret initiation to men of our own time, and while its methods and its practical achievements remain secrets in their hands, it is open to any patient and earnest student of the question to satisfy himself that these methods are of supreme efficacy, and these achievements far more admirable than any yet standing to the credit of modern science.

For the secrecy in which these operations have been shrouded has never disguised their existence, and it is only in our own time that this has been forgotten. Formerly at great public ceremonies, the initiates displayed the powers with which their knowledge of natural laws invested them. We carelessly assume that the narratives of such displays describe performances of magic. we have decided that there is no such thing as magic, therefore, the narratives must have been false, the persons whom they refer to, impostors. But, supposing that magic of old was simply the science of magi, of learned men, there is no magic, in the modern sense, left in the matter. And supposing that such science — even in ancient times already the product of long ages of study — had gone in some directions further than our much younger modern science has yet reached, it is reasonable to conclude that some displays in connection with ancient mysteries may have been strictly scientific experiments, though they sound like displays of magic, and would look like displays of magic for us now if they could be repeated.

On that hypothesis, modern sagacity applying modern knowledge to the subject of ancient mysteries may be merely modern folly evolving erroneous conclusions from modern ignorance.

But there is no need to construct hypotheses in the Matter. The facts are accessible if they are sought for in the right way, and the facts are these. The wisdom of the ancient world — science and religion commingled, physics and metaphysics combined — was a reality, and it still survives. It is that which will be spoken of in the teachings of the Church of Illuminism as Occult Philosophy. It was already a complete system of knowledge that had been cultivated in secret, and handed down to initiates for ages, before its professors performed experiments in public to impress the popular mind in Egypt and Greece. Adepts of occultism in the present day are capable of performing similar experiments, and of exhibiting results that prove them immeasurably further advanced than ordinary modern science in a comprehension of the forces of Nature. Furthermore, they inherit from their great predecessors a science which deals not merely with physics, but with the constitution and

capacities of the human soul and spirit.
Modern science has discovered the circulation
of the blood, occult science understands the
circulation of the life-principle. Modern
physiology deals with the body only,
occultism with the soul as well — not as the
subject of vague, religious rhapsodies, but as
an actual entity, with properties that can be
examined in combination with, or apart from,
those of the body.

It IS chiefly in the East that occultism is still
kept up — in India and in adjacent countries.
It is in India that we have encountered it, and
the Church of Illuminism is set up to describe
these experiences to you and to retail the
knowledge acquired, if you so seek it.